Illustrated COMPREHENSION

A complete book for competent and enthusiastic readers

5

INCLUDES

- Poetry Comprehensions
- Enhanced Vocabulary
- Grammar Exercises
- Creative Writing
- Multiple Choice Questions (MCQs)

MANOJ PUBLICATIONS

Publisher:
MANOJ PUBLICATIONS
761, Main Road, Burari, Delhi-110084 (INDIA)
Mobile: 09999476076, 9868112194
8178823569, 8178854810
Email: info@manojpublications.com
For online shopping visit our Website :
www.sawanonlinebookstore.com

ISBN : 978-93-91460-68-6

Illustrated Comprehension - 5

Conceived by : **Sanyam Gupta**
Written by : **Prashant Gupta**
Edited by : **Rohan Kumar**

Preface

Reading is a multifaceted process that develops only with practice. There are certain aspects of reading, such as fluency and word recognition, which can be learnt in a certain amount of time. These basics must be mastered but at the same time reading comprehension should be emphasized in the process. Students can parrot words on a page all day long, but if they don't have the necessary comprehension skills, they will not be able to make predictions, monitor their understanding of content, sequence or characters, clarify the confusing text, or connect what they're reading to their own experience or prior knowledge. And that is what true comprehension is all about.

The **Illustrated Comprehension** series designed for readers of grades 1 to 6 offers reading passages with questions on a variety of topics. The main objective is to lay the foundation to build up students' confidence in tackling comprehension, to encourage higher-level thinking and understanding, and also motivate to think beyond the ideas presented in the passages or poems. It will also help them enhance their **Word Power and Grammar Skills**.

We hope the present series will prove a boon for all the students and come up to their expectations.

Suggestions for the betterment of the series are welcomed.

– Publishers

Contents

S. No.	Chapter Name	Page No.
1.	Good Manners	5
2.	Reading a Newspaper	12
3.	Health is Wealth	17
4.	Mom (Poem)	23
5.	Overcoming The Examination Stress	27
6.	Presence of Mind	33
7.	Show the Earth You Care (Poem)	39
8.	Carefulness is the Key to Safety	45
9.	Florence Nightingale	51
10.	Politeness	56
11.	Dreams (Poem)	62
12.	Value of Good Health	68
13.	Obedience	73
14.	The True Meaning of Life (Poem)	79
15.	Admitting Our Faults	85
16.	Advantages of the Cinema	90
17.	Trust	96
18.	Steadfast Heart (Poem)	102
19.	Discipline Builds a Nation	108
20.	Home	114
21.	Adventures (Poem)	120
22.	Cooperation	124
23.	Olympic Granny (Poem)	129
24.	My Shadow (Poem)	135
	Answers	140

1 Good Manners

Manners make man perfect and complete. Good manners are **admired** by one and all. They make a person a useful member of the society. They lend colour and grace to our life. They make the life run smoothly. Good manners are even more important than the laws of the state.

We should have good manners at home. We should be respectful to our elders and **affectionate** to those who are younger than us. We should cooperate with each other in doing household works.

Good manners should be observed at school as well. We should be respectful to our teachers. We should not make a **mischief** in the class. We should not damage the school property. We should be helpful to weak students.

Good manners are equally important in social life. We should be courteous and polite to others. In no case should we lose our **temper**. We should be polite even while turning down the unfair request of others. We should treat all as equal. We should not hurt the feelings of others. Whenever somebody does us a favour, we should thank him/her.

Know These Words

admired	-	regarded with respect
affectionate	-	showing love for someone or something
mischief	-	bad behaviour
temper	-	state of mind

Questions-Answers

A. Underline the correct answer.

1. We should be courteous and ________ to others.

   a. polite b. cool c. harsh

2. We should treat all as __________.

   a. different b. inferior c. equal

3. Good manners are even more important than the ___________.

   a. law of the state b. personality c. smartness

4. To whom should we be affectionate?

   a. Our youngsters b. Our elders c. Our dear ones

B. Answer the following questions.

1. What do manners make a person?

____

____

____

2. To whom should we be respectful?

____

____

____

3. In what should we cooperate with each other?

4. Where should also good manners be observed?

5. When should we be polite?

6. When should we thank a person?

Creative Writing

C. Do you use the magic words 'Please, Thank you, and Sorry' in your conversation?

D. How do you react when someone speaks loudly to you? Do you manage to stay calm and respectful?

Word Power

E. Solve the crossword puzzle using the hints. Choose words from the Word Bank.

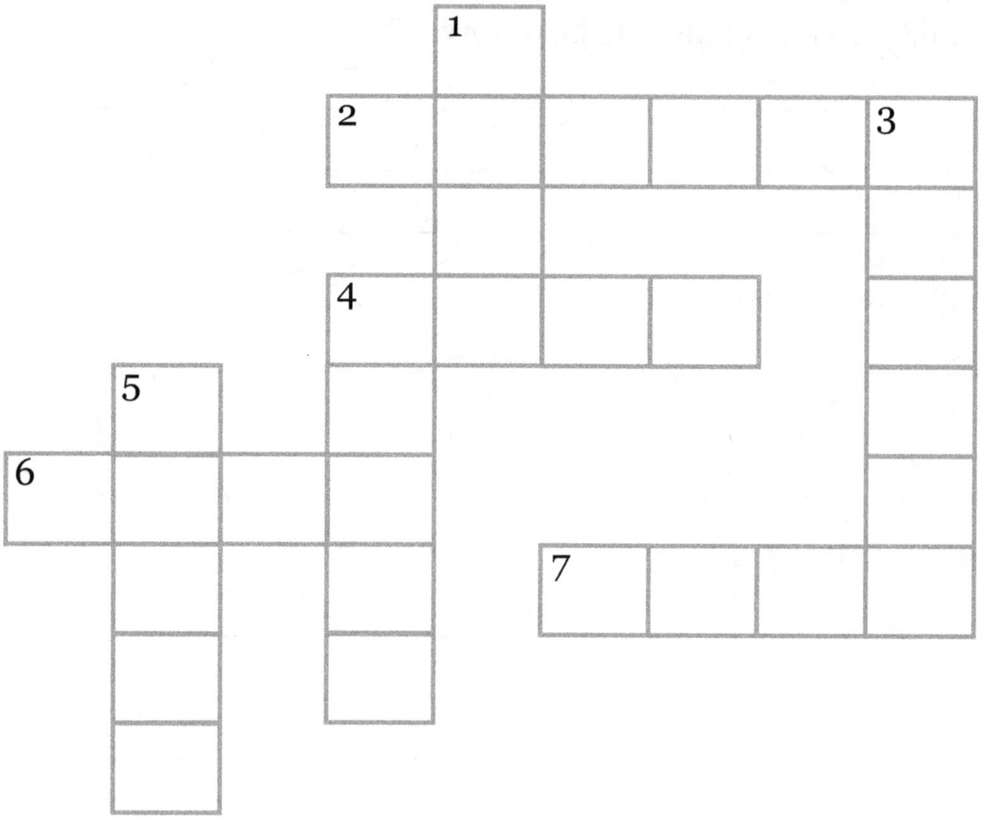

Across

2. A need for food
4. To be humble in spirit or manner
6. Having little money or a few possessions
7. To feel happiness, joy and pleasure

Down

1. To be without any faults ; without sin
3. A payment received in return for doing deeds
4. To show great kindness towards others
5. To feel sadness

Word Bank

pure	mourn	reward	hunger
poor	glad	mercy	meek

Grammar Skills

The Sentence

A sentence is a group of words that conveys a complete meaning. Some important types of sentences are discussed below.

- **Declarative sentences** express or describe some idea or thought in a straight, impersonal and objective way.

  For example : The television-set operates on 220 volts.

  (Such a sentence generally ends with a full stop.)

- **An imperative sentence** gives command. It usually ends with a full stop. Commands ask or tell people to do something.

  For example : Harry, call me now.

  Please bring me a cup of tea.

- **An exclamatory sentence** expresses different kinds of emotions such as command, request, desire or wish. It ends with an exclamation mark.

  For example : How beautiful you look in this dress!

- **An interrogative sentence** always asks a question. It ends in a question mark (?).

  For example : Is the shop open today?

- **A negative sentence** states the negation of an action; 'no' or 'not' or 'never' is used in the sentence.

  For example : The school is not open today.

F. Change the sentences as directed.

1. This computer is working. (Declarative)

   a. ______________________________ (Change into interrogative)

   b. ______________________________ (Change into negative)

   c. ______________________________ (Change into exclamatory)

2. The buses are not running today. (Negative)

a. ______________________________ (Change into interrogative)

b. ______________________________ (Change into declarative)

c. ______________________________ (Change into exclamatory)

3. Hold my bag. (Imperative)

a. ______________________________ (Change into negative)

b. ______________________________ (Change into declarative)

c. ______________________________ (Change into interrogative)

4. Are you feeling sick? (Interrogative)

a. ______________________________ (Change into declarative)

b. ______________________________ (Change into exclamatory)

c. ______________________________ (Change into negative)

G. Change these groups of words into meaningful sentences by adding some words to them.

1. The teachers are ____.
2. Switch ____.
3. There are ____.
4. My father was ____.
5. When did you ____?

Let us Know More

Good manners are very important in our daily life. They are required to create an effective interaction with friends as well as to make a good impression on them. They help us to remain positive throughout the day. We must use the magic words like 'sorry', 'please', 'thank you', 'excuse me', etc., whenever required without delay in order to maintain a happy relationship. Good manners open the doors to new areas and opportunities in life. If someone talks to you rudely, be calm and behave nicely so that the other person may realise his mistake. Our good character reflects in our good manners.

Fun Chat

Do you know that some of our most familiar etiquette rules have long and surprising histories?

Saying 'Bless You' after sneezes

This practice dates back to at least 590 CE when Pope Gregory I commanded that anyone who sneezed immediately be blessed in hope that the prayer would protect him/her from an otherwise certain death.

Shaking hands

Shaking hands upon greeting was originally adopted several centuries ago in England as a means of establishing that neither party was armed.

Not pointing at someone

Almost all cultures throughout history and around the world consider it to be rude to point at someone. It's difficult to pinpoint an exact origin of this belief, but many explanations centre on the ancient idea that you could transfer evil sprits to someone by staring at him/her with negative thoughts in your mind, a so-called 'evil eye'. By pointing at someone, you direct attention and possibly 'evil eyes' at them.

2 Reading a Newspaper

Reading a newspaper has become a necessity in the modern times. The world today appears to be smaller than it was in the 19th century. Newspapers do us a great service by bringing news from every corner of the world. We feel as if it has happened in our **neighbourhood**.

A newspaper caters to the needs of various sections of the society. A politician finds the news and reviews of others on the policy adopted by the government of a political party. A businessman can find the trends of the market and advertise his goods. A job-**seeker** can find a suitable job through 'Situations Vacant' column. A sports fan gets the latest information about his favourite game being played in any part of the world. We come to know about the weather forecast through newspapers. In brief, a daily newspaper contains all information that a person needs.

While reading newspapers, we should **be on guard**. Sometimes newspapers become willing tools in the hands of **vested** interests. They do not place true facts before the public. So we should prefer independent views and reviews while reading them.

Know These Words

neighbourhood	-	a district or community within a city or town
seeker	-	one who searches for something
be on guard	-	be careful
vested	-	fully and unconditionally guaranteed as a legal right

Questions-Answers

A. Underline the correct answer.

1. What has become a necessity in the modern times?
   a. Reading a newspaper
   b. Using the Internet
   c. Watching TV
2. Newspapers do not place __________ facts before the public.
   a. funny b. false c. true
3. We come to know about the __________ through the newspaper.
   a. weather b. seasons c. temperature
4. In which column can a job-seeker find a job in the newspaper?
   a. Jobs and Jobs b. Situations Vacant c. Vacancies

B. Answer the following questions.

1. What service do newspapers do for us?

   ____

   ____

2. What does a politician get from the newspaper?

   ____

   ____

3. What does a sports fan get from the newspaper?

   ____

   ____

4. What do newspapers become sometimes?

5. What should we prefer while reading the newspaper and why?

Creative Writing

C. Do you read the newspaper every day? What type of information do you like to read in it?

D. How do newspapers help us to increase our knowledge in daily routine life?

Word Power

E. Match the Columns:

Column I	Column II
1. heading or title at the top of page	a. horoscope
2. news printed in a vertical box	b. weather report
3. a section about star signs and zodiac signs	c. business section
4. a section for weather forecast	d. special feature
5. a section with business news	e. column
6. a special story	f. headlines

Grammar Skills

Subject and Predicate

A sentence can be divided into two parts— **Subject** and **Predicate**.

The part of the sentence which tells what the sentence is about is the **subject**.

The part of the sentence which says something about the subject is the **predicate**.

For example:

Sophia / lives in a big house.

↓ ↓

Subject **Predicate**

In this sentence, '**Sophia**' is the subject of the sentence. The words '**lives in a big house**' say something about Sophia. Thus, 'lives in a big house' is the predicate of the sentence.

F. Match the subjects with their predicates :

Column A	**Column B**
1. All insects	a. heard the telephone bell ringing.
2. Children	b. are hard-working people.
3. A good student	c. have six legs.
4. None of us	d. halt at these small stations.
5. Life in the hills	e. can be tiring.
6. Indian farmers	f. is always punctual.
7. Very few trains	g. are fond of asking questions.
8. A long train journey	h. has its own charms.

G. Write the subjects in the following sentences.

1. ______________________ shed their leaves in winter.
2. ______________________ falls on 5th October.
3. A ______________________ has long pink ears.
4. ______________________ becomes pleasant in spring.
5. ______________________ take care of your health.

Let us Know More

1. Reading news helps you to develop an open and critical mind.
2. Reading news is a source of inspiration, knowledge and finding solutions.
3. Reading news can enhance your creativity.
4. Reading news helps you to improve your storytelling techniques.
5. Reading news helps you to improve your language skills.

Fun Chat

Mom : Zubair, have you seen my newspaper?

Zubair : Mom, newspapers are old school! Why don't you use a tablet instead?

Mom : Am I supposed to use the tablet to kill a fly?

☺ ☺ ☺

3 Health is Wealth

Once upon a time, there was a king who was very lazy. He did not like to do anything. He waited for his **attendants** to serve him every moment. He used to lie on his bed always. Then a time came when he totally became inactive.

Eating good food and sleeping made him fat. He became so fat that he could not move around by himself. He felt sick. Doctors were called in to treat him. None could help him to become fit and fine again. The king was a kind-hearted and **cordial** person. All people living there were sorry to learn about the fact that their king was not well.

One day the minister met a holy man (Sadhu) on the outskirts of the city. While conversing with him, the Sadhu came to know that the king was unwell.

He told the minister that he could cure the king. Hearing this the minister's face brightened. He arranged immediately for a meeting of the Sadhu and the king.

The Sadhu saw the depressed king for a while and then spoke that nothing serious had happened and that the king would be all right. From the next day the treatment would start. He asked the king to come to his hut which was at a distance from the palace.

The king had to come on foot to the hut. The king agreed. After so many years the king had come outside to walk on the road. His ministers and attendants **accompanied** him. By the time he reached the Sadhu's hut, he was breathless, sweating and uncomfortable. The Sadhu came out of the hut noticing everything. He offered cool water to the king. The king felt better. The Sadhu brought out an iron ball, the size of a football and gave it to the attendants asking His Majesty that every day morning and evening he had to roll that ball in the palace ground.

The king agreed and the Sadhu left the city. After fifteen days when the Sadhu came to the palace to meet the king, the king had lost a considerable amount of weight, was feeling much better and was active. All his sickness had disappeared.

Know These Words

attendants	-	persons who attend; servants
cordial	-	warm and friendly
accompanied	-	went somewhere with someone

Questions-Answers

A. Underline the correct answer.

1. Who didn't like to do anything?

   a. King b. Attendants c. Minister

2. Who was called in to treat the king?

   a. Sadhu b. Doctors c. Ministers

3. What was the ball made up of?

a. Iron　　b. Plastic　　c. Rubber

4. How many days later did the Sadhu come to the palace to meet the king?

a. 10 days　　b. 20 days　　c. 15 days

B. Answer the following questions.

1. Why did the king not like to do anything?

____

____

2. Why did the king wait for his attendants every moment?

____

____

3. What made the king fat?

____

____

4. What did the holy man come to know?

____

____

5. What did the holy man tell the minister?

____

____

6. What did the holy man bring out and give to the attendants?

____

____

7. What did the Sadhu ask His Majesty?

____

____

8. What did the holy man see after fifteen days?

____

____

Creative Writing

C. Are you a lazy child? Do you think it is good to eat and sleep a lot without doing any physical exercise?

____

____

____

____

____

____

D. Being active is necessary for everyone. What exercise should one do to remain active?

____

____

____

____

____

____

Grammar Skills

Parts of Speech

The words that we speak or write can be divided into nine parts called parts of speech. These are:

Noun	Pronoun	Adjective
Determiner	Verb	Adverb
Preposition	Conjunction	Interjection

Noun : A noun names a person, place, an animal or a thing.

Pronoun : A pronoun is a word used in place of a noun.

Adjective : An adjective tells us something about a noun or pronoun.

Determiner : A determiner determines a noun. It just precedes of the noun.

Verb : A verb tells us what persons, animals or things do. It is used for showing 'doing', 'being' or 'possession'.

Adverb : An adverb tells us more about a verb, another adverb or adjective.

Preposition : A preposition shows the relation between a noun, pronoun or some other words in a sentence.

Conjunction : A conjunction helps to join words or a group of words.

Interjection : An interjection expresses a sudden feeling.

In order to understand the part of speech a word belongs to, we should understand the work it does in a sentence.

For example:

Interjection	Pronoun	Conjunction	Determiner	Noun	Verb	Determiner	Adjective
↓	↓	↓	↓	↓	↓	↓	↓
Hurrah!	I	and	my	friends	solved	the	difficult

Noun	Adverb	Conjunction	Verb	Determiner	Adjective	Preposition	Determiner	Noun
↓	↓	↓	↓	↓	↓	↓	↓	↓
problem	easily,	and	scored	the	highest	in	the	quiz.

E. Name the parts of speech of the highlighted words.

1. My favourite fruit is strawberry. ________________ ________________
2. Johnson is her friend. ________________ ________________
3. My mother works in a hospital. ________________ ________________
4. The frog jumped into the big pond. ________________ ________________
5. Heena sang and danced gracefully. ________________ ________________

F. Underline the prepositions, the conjunctions and the interjections in the sentences given below.

1. Sure! We will watch blue whales, dolphins and other sea creatures.

   ____

2. Owls turn their heads almost a complete circle but they cannot move their eyes.

   ____

3. We saw a large number of animals in the zoo.

   ____

Let us Know More

Obesity is the biggest problem our country is facing now. Children are falling prey to obesity faster than expected. However, this can still be controlled. Obese people usually indulge in a lot of junk food which contains sugar, salt and fats which contribute to obesity. Healthy food can help you get rid of all this as it does not contain harmful things. In addition, healthy food also helps you save money. It is much cheaper in comparison to junk food. Thus, you will be saving a great amount when you consume only healthy food.

Fun Chat

Read the jokes and laugh aloud.

Man : Waiter, will my pizza be long?

Waiter : No sir; it will be round.

☺ ☺ ☺

Mom : When do you go at red and stop at green?

Son : When I'am eating a watermelon!!

☺ ☺ ☺

4 Mom

You are the sunlight in my day,
You are the moon that shines every day.
You are the tree I **lean** upon,
You are the one who makes my troubles be gone,

You are the one who taught me life,
How not to fight and what is right.
You are the words inside my song.
You are my **wonderful** mom.

You are the one who cares for me,
You are the eyes that help me see.
You are the one who knows me best.
When it's time to have fun and time to rest.
You are the one who helps me dream,
You are my heart,

You hear my **screams**.
Afraid of life but looking for love,
I'm **blessed**, for God sent me you from above,
You are my friend, my heart and my soul,
You are the greatest Mom I know.

Know These Words

lean	-	*to take suport*
wonderful	-	extremely good
screams	-	shouts
blessed	-	lucky; fortunate

Questions-Answers

A. Fill in the blanks.

1. Mom is the ________ we can lean upon.
2. Mom is the one who makes our ______________ gone.
3. Mom is the ___________ inside our song.
4. __________ is the one who __________ for us.
5. Mom is the one who knows us ___________ .
6. __________ is the one who helps us __________ .

B. Answer the following questions.

1. To whom does the poet compare his mom in the first line?

____

2. What does mom tell us about life?

____

3. What does mom hear without saying?

____

4. What is the poet afraid of ?

____

5. What is the poet looking for?

____

6. Why does the poet feel blessed?

____

7. Write two adjectives used for describing mom.

____

Creative Writing

C. Write a few lines about your mom. How does she take care of you?

____

____

D. What do you do for your mom?

____

____

Grammar Skills

Noun

- A noun is the name of a person, place, an action, a quality, feeling, an idea or a thing.

Proper Noun

- The name of a particular person, place, animal or thing.
- Begins with a capital letter

For example :

Person - Mr Robot

Animal - Sheru

Place - North America

Thing - Pride and Prejudice (Name of a novel)

Common Noun

- The name of any person, place, animal or thing.
- Does not begin with a capital letter.
- Also known as a **general** noun.

For example :

Person - Girl

Place - City

Animal - Cat

Thing - Television-set

Collective Noun

- A collection or group of persons, places, animals or things.

  For example :

a **flock** of birds	a cricket **team**
a **family**	a **herd**

E. Underline the noun in each sentence. Write whether the noun is common, proper or collective.

1. Miss Suzie always cleans the house. ____________
2. The excited team celebrated the victory. ____________
3. We all love a long drive on Sundays. ____________
4. He climbed Mount Everest. ____________
5. I love my adorable puppy. ____________
6. The colony of ants was travelling North. ____________
7. Joseph cried miserably. ____________
8. She lives on Jonson Street. ____________
9. The band played beautifully. ____________
10. The houses were decorated with lights. ____________

Let us Know More

"God could not be everywhere, and therefore he made mothers." Mother is a very special and important person for every child. In fact, she is the most precious gift of God for everyone. A child can see the world only because of her. She is a friend, parent, guide and teacher to her child. She takes care of the entire family and turns a house into a beautiful home. She brings up her children with utmost care, compassion and love. She illuminates our homes with her presence and smile. We can say that mother is not simply a word; it is a whole universe in itself.

Fun Chat

Kid : Mom, give me some money. I want to help the poor.

Mother came outside and didn't find anyone.

Mother : Where are the poor?

Kid : Look over there; the poor fellow is selling ice cream in the scorching sun!

☺ ☺ ☺

5 Overcoming the Examination Stress

Stress is **part and parcel** of our life. Everyone experiences stress from time to time. Perhaps the most stressful time for students is when an examination approaches. A great tension from their teachers and parents stresses students to do well in the exam.

Stress at the time of an examination is often the result of lack of **self-confidence**. Those who are not well prepared for the exam suffer from **anxiety** and fear of failure. Those are probably the students who do not study regularly and leave revision for the last minute.

There are many ways to minimize the examination stress. The starting point is to be attentive in the class as this is the most effective way of learning and understanding a particular subject. Students should also be **consistent** in doing their homework and study steadily throughout the year without waiting for the exam.

Students should pay more attention to subjects in which they are weak. Parents should help them and monitor their progress in such subjects. If necessary, they can arrange a tutor for their children to help them.

Many students make the mistake of doing revision in the last minute. Revision should be done regularly so that work may not get piled up. Consistent revision helps build confidence. Confident students tend to do well in examinations.

Know These Words

part and parcel	-	necessary part
self-confidence	-	having trust in oneself
anxiety	-	a feeling of worry
consistent	-	continuous

Questions-Answers

A. Underline the correct answer.

1. The most stressful time for a student is when an ______ approaches.

   a. result b. annual day c. examination

2. The students who are ______ for the exam suffer from anxiety and fear of failure.

   a. well prepared b. not well prepared c. confident

3. ______________ students tend to do well in the examination.

   a. Confident b. Intelligent c. Weak

B. Answer the following questions.

1. What is the most stressful time for students?

____

____

____

2. What great tension stresses students to do well in the exam?

____

____

____

3. Who are the students that suffer from the anxiety and fear of failure?

____

____

____

4. What is the starting point to minimize the stress?

5. What should students do throughout the year?

6. What should be done regularly and why?

7. What should parents do?

Creative Writing

C. Do you revise your lessons every day or you wait for your exams to study well?

D. Do you feel stressed when an examination approaches? What should one do to minimize one's stress?

Word Power

E. Solve the crossword puzzle using the hints.

1. Someone who is taking an examination is called ______________.
2. An official document stating that you have passed an examination, successfully completed a course in a particular profession is called ______________.
3. An important test of your knowledge, especially the one that you take at school is called ______________.
4. Someone whose job is to test people's knowledge or ability is called ______________.
5. The paper that you write your answers on in an examination is called ______________.
6. Question containing several answers from which you have to choose the correct one is called a ______________.

Grammar Skills

Nouns

Abstract Noun

An abstract noun is the name of some quality, feeling or idea which we can only think of or feel, but can never touch or see.

For example:

Birbal is known for his **wit** and **wisdom**.

Countable and Uncountable nouns

The nouns which can be counted are **countable** nouns.

For example:

She drinks two **cups** of coffee in the morning.

The nouns which cannot be counted are **uncountable** nouns.

For example:

She drinks **coffee** in the morning.

F. Match the following abstract nouns.

1. A dishonest man	a. anger
2. A foolish person	b. cowardice
3. An angry neighbour	c. innocence
4. A high monument	d. growth
5. A cowardly soldier	e. foolishness
6. A free bird	f. death
7. A growing child	g. happiness
8. A happy woman	h. freedom
9. A dead rat	i. height
10. An innocent girl	j. dishonesty

G. Write C for a countable noun and U for an uncountable noun.

1. key	◯	2. soap	◯	3. air	◯
4. box	◯	5. brick	◯	6. flowers	◯
7. pans	◯	8. water	◯	9. slice	◯
10. rain	◯				

Let us Know More

Studying and preparing is vital to success in exams.

Some of these points sound like 'common sense' and relate to the importance of looking after yourself during your preparation.

1. Start your revision early.
2. Organise your study time.
3. Look after yourself during study and exam time. You will be able to work better if you eat a healthy diet, and get proper sleep.
4. Vary your revision techniques. They say that variety is the spice of life, and it certainly helps to improve the way you study.
5. Take regular breaks.
   You cannot work solidly for 8 hours. In fact, it is very hard to work in a concentrated way for more than two hours. So, take short breaks.

Fun Chat

Read the jokes and laugh aloud.

Teacher : How was the paper?

Student : It was easy but question No. 5 confused me.

Teacher : What was the question?

Student : Question No. 5 wanted the past tense of 'Think'; I thought and thought and ended up with writing 'thinked'.

☺ ☺ ☺

6 Presence of Mind

Once, there lived a **wise** farmer in a village. He had a small farm at some distance from his village. He had sown carrots. One day, he was working on his farm with his servants. Suddenly, he heard the **growl** of a bear. As he turned around, he saw a wild bear standing close to him. For a moment, he got **scared** but he did not lose his presence of mind. He summed up his courage and said, "Good morning, Mr Bear. I welcome you to my farm. Let me know what I can do for you, sir."

"You have such a big farm and have grown a lot of things here, but you give me nothing to eat. It seems you are selfish. Now I will **destroy** your farm," said the bear.

"Don't do that, please," said the farmer to the bear, "My family depends completely on this farm for a living. If you destroy it, we will all die of hunger. I am sorry I haven't given you anything before. But I am ready to give you a share now."

"But how much will my share be?" asked the bear. "I shall give you half the crop, sir!" said the farmer.

"But what will you give me?" asked the bear.

The farmer replied, "I am ready to give you all the tops and I'll have only the roots for myself."

The bear agreed to this proposal and said, "All right; call me when the crop is ready. Now I am going to the forest. Be careful; if you fail to call me, I shall not spare you." After saying this, the bear went into the forest.

After a few months, when the carrots were **ripe** for harvest, the bear reached there on his own. The wise farmer gave the bear all the leaves and kept the carrots for himself. He put them into his cart and left for home.

By chance, a few carrots slipped off the cart and fell on the ground. The bear picked up a carrot out of **curiosity** and had a bite. It was very tasty and juicy. Then, he tasted the leaves. They had no taste at all. He said to himself, "The farmer has cheated me. I would have to teach him a lesson." The bear ran after the farmer's cart and soon overtook it.

"You have befooled me," said the bear in his angry voice, "You've kept all the roots for yourself and gave me the useless things, their leaves. Now listen; next time I shall have the roots and you will have the leaves."

"All right, sir," the farmer agreed. Next time, the farmer **sowed** wheat. When the crop was ripe, the bear reached there again and said, "Give me my share."

"You can have all the roots; I want the tops only." The farmer cut all the ears off the stalks, put them into his cart and left for home.

The bear was very happy. He said to himself, "This time, I have befooled the farmer. I shall enjoy the sweet roots." He never knew that the intelligent farmer had again outwitted him. If the farmer had lost his presence of mind and had not used his wit, he would have been killed by the bear. When you are in trouble or distress, never lose **patience**. Don't you know that God helps those who help themselves? Remember, only those who deal with the problems calmly and without haste, attain success. God has given us a unique power of thinking and wisdom. We are the best among all the creatures.

Know These Words

wise	-	knowledgeable, intelligent
growl	-	to make a low noise in the throat to show anger
scared	-	frightened

destroy	-	ruin, tear down
ripe	-	(of fruit or grain) developed to the point of readiness for harvesting and eating
curiosity	-	a strong desire to know
sowed	-	planted seeds by scattering them on/in the earth
patience	-	the ability to wait

Questions-Answers

A. Underline the correct answer.

1. What had the farmer sowed in his farm?
   a. Radish b. Carrots c. Pumpkin
2. Who is said to be selfish in the story?
   a. Farmer b. Bear c. Both a and b
3. What were very tasty and juicy?
   a. Wheat b. Carrots c. Leaves
4. What did the farmer sow the second time?
   a. Wheat b. Beans c. Carrots

B. Answer the following questions.

1. What did the bear say to the farmer when he met him the first time?

   ____

   ____

2. What did the farmer say to the bear about his family?

   ____

   ____

3. On what condition did the bear agree not to destroy the crop of carrots?

   ____

   ____

4. What did the farmer give the bear the first time and what did he keep with him?

5. How did the bear realise that the farmer had cheated him?

6. What did the farmer give the bear next time?

7. What had happened if the farmer would have lost his presence of mind?

Creative Writing

C. How do you react when someone threatens you to take away your belongings?

D. Write about any situation where you saved yourself from an accident due to the presence of your mind.

Word Power

E. Can you find the correct word for each jumbled word?

1. y e s s a ____________________
2. l i f a ____________________
3. r u s e l t ____________________
4. t s t e ____________________
5. n a t i o n e m a x i ____________________
6. c p r o j e t ____________________
7. q l i y u a f ____________________
8. a r m k s ____________________
9. s s a p ____________________
10. e r a g d ____________________

Grammar Skills

Use of a, an, some, any

- A is used with a singular countable noun that begins with a consonant.
- An is used with a singular countable noun that begins with a vowel.
- Some can be used with a plural countable noun or singular uncountable noun. It is usually used in a positive statement.
- Any is usually used with a plural countable noun or a singular uncountable noun. It is usually used in a question or negative statement.

F. Fill in each blank with a, an, some or any.

1. Look! There is ________ tiny mouse in the cage.
2. Excuse me; is there ________ computer free?
3. I didn't have ________ ice cream. I had ________ pack of crisps.
4. They said it was ________ easy exercise.
5. I haven't got ________ oil left. Can you lend me ________?

6. Did you get ________ information at the desk?
7. Good morning! I'd like ________ bread.
8. My city is ________ wonderful place to live in.
9. There is ________ cheese on the table.
10. Is there ________ orange in the bowl?

Let us Know More

Train Your Brain

Do you know how playing certain types of games can help you get better concentration?

Try these games

- Sudoku
- Crossword puzzles
- Chess
- Jigsaw puzzles
- Word searches
- Scrambles
- Memory games

Fun Chat

The kids in a cafeteria of a school were lined up for lunch. At the head of the table was a large pile of fruits. The teacher made a note and pasted on the fruit tray.

'Take only ONE. God is watching.'

Moving further along the lunch line, at the other end of the table was a large pile of chocolate chip cookies.

A child wrote a note, "Take all you want. God is watching the fruits."

7 Show the Earth You Care

When you see **litter** in the streets
And the air smells of pollution,
When you feel like it's all **piling up**
Remember there is a solution.

There's something each of us can do
To keep the rivers clean
To keep fresh, the air we breathe
And keep the **forests** green.

Help clean a beach
Or **recycle** bottles and cans
Learn about the problems we face
And help others understand.

It doesn't have to be a lot
If we each just do our share
so take time out on each day
To show the Earth you care.

Know These Words

litter - garbage

piling up - forming a heap

forests - jungle

recycle - reprocess; reuse

Questions-Answers

A. Fill in the blanks with the suitable words.

1. We can help keep the ________ clean.
2. We can help keep the ________fresh.
3. We can help keep the ________ green.
4. We should recycle ________ and ________.

B. Answer the following questions.

1. What is the poem about?

____

____

2. What should we remember when there is a pollution around us?

____

____

3. What should we help others understand?

____

____

4. How can the Earth be pollution-free?

____

____

5. Which word in the poem has the same meaning as 'garbage'?

6. Find three verbs from the poem.

7. Use the phrase 'take time out' in your own sentence.

8. What should we recycle? Name two things from the poem and two things other than those mentioned in the poem.

Creative Writing

C. You are in a park with your friends. You and your friends ate chocolates and your friends threw wrappers on the ground. How will you react? What will you do or say to your friends?

D. What do you do with the empty bottles and cans at home?

Word Power

E. Solve the crossword puzzle.

1. What liquid do we drink most of the time?
2. What is polluted water called?
3. to remove water
4. our surroundings
5. They cause water pollution
6. It harms lakes and rivers
7. main sources of water pollution
8. gases that are produced from vehicles
9. plants and animals that live in water

Grammar Skills

Verb

A verb is used for saying or asserting something about a person or thing. It says what a person or thing does, what a person or thing is, or what a person or thing has. A verb denotes 'doing', 'being' or 'possessing'.

For example:

Birds **fly** in the sky.
The shopkeeper **cheated** me. (doing)

Monica **is** a sweet girl.
Father **was** angry with me. (being)

A car **has** four wheels.
She **had** six oranges. (Possessing)

Transitive verb : A verb that requires an object to make sense is called a transitive verb.

For example : Mary **laughed** at the beggar. He **kicked** the ball.

Intransitive verb : A verb that does not require an object to make sense by itself is called an **intransitive** verb.

For example : Mary **laughed**. He **kicked**.

F. Identify the highlighted verb as transitive **or** intransitive **in each of the following sentences.**

1. She **delivered** the cake at my home. ____________
2. Her mother finally **delivered**. ____________
3. The children **played** a prank on him. ____________
4. Finally, we all **played**. ____________
5. We shall **continue** the meeting after the break. ____________
6. The meeting **continued** after the break. ____________
7. The students **play** the guitar. ____________
8. The students will **play** outside. ____________
9. Zoya **returned** the book to the library. ____________
10. The students **returned** to school. ____________
11. She is **drinking** milk from the bottle. ____________
12. The horse is **drinking**. ____________

G. Write the correct form of the verb to complete each sentence.

1. Kelvin couldn't read or __________ (writes/write)
2. Many people __________ (was/were) taking part in the procession.
3. This 50-rupee note __________ (appear/appears) to be fake.
4. Either my friend or my classmate __________ (is/are) taking me for a movie.
5. Some students __________ (seem/seems) to be missing from the class.

Let us Know More

We can recycle almost all of our garbage. Recycling not only saves valuable space in our landfills, but also it helps reduce greenhouse gas emissions.

Look at the list of common household items you can recycle.

- Recycle the empty envelopes that remain once you have opened your mail.
- Donate or sell any books that you no longer read. Keep in mind that outdated books can still have a life on Amazon and Bay.
- Recycle cardboard boxes, including cereal boxes, pizza boxes, cracker boxes, and any other types of package.
- Do you have a lot of old charges and power cords at home? Do not throw them away. Find recycling centres in your area that accept computer components and power cords.

Fun Chat

- Experts estimate that the Americans use about 500 million plastic straws a day, and they're one of the top 10 trash items found during ocean clean-ups. If you must use a straw, find a resusable metal straw or a paper version or make your own.
- Don't fill your birthday goodie bags with plastic yo-yos and other trinkets for your friends. Instead, give them homemade treats.
- Form a club in your classroom to reduce your waste at school. Monitor what's thrown away each week, and think about ways to cut down on those items.

8 Carefulness is the Key to Safety

In today's era, road accidents are **rampant**. A number of deaths occur as a result of these accidents. Accidents are responsible for a lot of injuries, both serious or **minor**. In many cases, these accidents could have been prevented if the people had just been a bit more careful. A few people among us think about safety.

Take road accidents, for example. The police say that most of the fatalities and injuries on roads are caused by the people driving their vehicles very fast. They do not observe their speed limits and make roads a dangerous place for all of us.

The police also say that the number of accidents could greatly be **reduced** if drivers concentrate more on their driving. Quite often, drivers have been thinking about their work problems, talking to co-passengers in the car, reading maps, eating snacks or even talking on mobile phones. In some countries, it is illegal to use a hand-held mobile phone while driving.

Pedestrians should also take care on roads to avoid accidents. It is important that they should cross at the pedestrian crossings wherever these are available. Where there are no pedestrian crossings, they should look both the sides before crossing the road to makes sure that no vehicle is coming from any side. Most of the people just rush across roads without paying much attention to this.

There is, unfortunately, a higher rate of accidents among cyclists on roads than cars. Cyclists can help themselves prevent these accidents by making themselves **visible** to motorists by wearing bright-coloured clothing and wear something reflective that can be seen in the dark. In order to lessen the effects of any injury, cyclists should always wear protective helmets for safety.

It is not only on roads that we should think of safety; great care should also be taken at home while doing household chores. Safety first indeed should be our motto all the time.

Know These Words

rampant	-	getting worse quickly and in an uncontrolled way
minor	-	lesser
reduced	-	made smaller
pedestrian (s)	-	a person who walks along the road
visible	-	that can be seen

Questions-Answers

A. Underline the correct answer.

1. What are rampant in today's era?
   a. Road accidents
   b. Home accidents
   c. Workplace accidents
2. How can accidents be prevented?
   a. By being careful
   b. By being careless
   c. By staying at home

3. Where should we look before crossing the road?

   a. Left side   b. Right side   c. Both the sides

4. Cyclists should always wear protective ________________.

   a. helmets   b. caps   c. hats

B. Answer the following questions.

1. Why do a number of deaths occur?

   ____

   ____

2. What do the police say about driving vehicles very fast?

   ____

   ____

3. How have drivers made roads a dangerous place?

   ____

   ____

4. How can the number of accidents be reduced?

   ____

   ____

5. What is illegal in some countries?

   ____

   ____

6. How can cyclists help prevent accidents?

   ____

   ____

7. Write the opposite of 'carefulness' and use both the words in your own sentences.

   ____

   ____

Creative Writing

C. Are you a careful child? Write any three things you take care of to be safe at every place.

____

____

____

____

D. Write any three consequences of carelessness you have faced.

____

____

____

____

Word Power

E. Find the synonyms of the word 'safe' in the word grid.

p	r	o	t	e	c	t	i	v	e	p	y
t	a	y	y	h	u	y	a	a	u	r	a
s	l	r	c	a	r	e	f	u	l	e	v
q	a	s	i	r	o	u	s	y	s	v	o
m	r	u	o	m	t	i	q	l	t	e	i
s	m	i	p	l	e	o	r	o	r	n	d
z	e	o	s	e	c	u	r	e	q	t	a
j	d	s	e	s	r	p	y	n	s	a	b
k	a	k	t	s	t	o	u	e	a	b	l
c	o	n	t	r	o	l	l	a	b	l	e
s	t	d	s	v	a	d	i	d	s	e	s

Word Bank				
	protective	alarmed	controllable	preventable
	avoidable	harmless	secure	careful

Grammar Skills

Pronouns

A pronoun is a word used in place of a noun.

Demonstrative Pronoun

The pronoun that points out or demonstrates persons or things is known as a **demonstrative pronoun**, such as **this**, **that**, **these** and **those**.

This and **these** are singular; they are used for people or things that are **near** the speaker.

That and **those** are plural; they are used for people or things that are **farther** away from the speaker.

For example:

1. **This** is a cake.
2. **These** are nice grapes. But they taste sour.
3. Look! **That** is a lovely aquarium.
4. **Those** are small fish in it.

F. Fill in the blanks with the appropriate demonstrative pronouns.

1. ____________ is my video game.
2. ____________ is Mr Fogg's bungalow.
3. ____________ is our classroom.
4. ____________ are the keys lying on the bed.
5. ____________ was incredible.
6. ____________ are her shoes.
7. Can you see? ____________ is a giant yellow board over there.
8. ____________ were not Sarah's files.

Let us Know More

Walking is a healthy activity, but you need to know the rules of thumb for pedestrian safety. To stay safe while walking, follow these rules of the road.

Do

- Pay attention to traffic.
- Walk on the sidewalk whenever possible.
- Walk on footpath.
- Remember that motorists might not see you.

Don't

- walk with your back to the oncoming traffic.
- forget to watch for other pedestrians and cyclists.
- wear dark-coloured clothing, especially at night.
- listen to loud music or look at your phone.

Fun Chat

Think before you answer this riddle.

A window cleaner is cleaning a window on the 25th floor of a skyscraper when, suddenly, he slips and falls.

He has no safety equipment and nothing to soften his fall, and yet he is not hurt.

How can this be possible?

9 Florence Nightingale

Florence Nightingale is among the personalities we always admired for her **tremendous** care and love, she showed to the sick and the poor.

Florence Nightingale was born to English parents in 1820. Her parents were there on a visit to the town of Florence in Italy at the time of her birth. So, they named her Florence. Soon after her birth, the family returned to England.

Florence never went to school. She was taught by her parents and a tutor at home. She grew up to be different from the other girls of her age, always thoughtful and serious. One of the things that **distressed** Florence was the suffering of the sick and the poor. She felt that God wanted her to **devote** her life to serving them.

Florence Nightingale is best known for her services during the Crimean war, which broke out in 1853. British soldiers had been sent to Crimea, in Eastern Europe, to fight against the Russians. Florence volunteered to go there with a group of nurses to take care of hundreds of soldiers **wounded** in the war.

In Crimea, Florence showed great devotion in looking

after the wounded. It was common to see her carrying an oil lamp and walking through wards to make sure they had attention, they needed. For this, she was named "The lady with the Lamp" and she earned great respect from her patients.

After the war, Florence Nightingale returned home. Back in England, she continued to contribute to nursing profession. She gave talks on nursing and founded Nightingale School of Nurses at St. Thomas' Hospital, London. Florence died in 1910 at the age of 90. Today, she continues to be a source of inspiration for nurses around the world.

Know These Words

tremendous	-	great in amount
distressed	-	troubled
devote	-	to give your time completely to something
wounded	-	injured or harmed seriously

Questions-Answers

A. Fill in the blanks.

1. Soon after Florence's birth, the family returned to __________.
2. Florence was __________ and __________.
3. Crimean war broke out in __________.
4. Florence gave talks on __________.
5. Florence founded __________ at St. Thomas' Hospital, London.

B. Answer the following questions.

1. When was Florence Nightingale born?

____

____

2. Why did her parents name her Florence?

____

____

3. What did Florence think about the poor and the sick?

4. For what is Florence Nightingale best known for?

5. Why did Florence go to the Eastern Europe?

6. What was common to see her with?

7. By what name was she famous?

8. Where did she give talks on nursing?

9. When did she die?

10. What does she continue to be today?

Creative Writing

C. Do you have an ideal? How is she/he a source of inspiration for you?

Word Power

D. Match each adjective with its opposite.

1. polite	a. lazy
2. outgoing	b. rude
3. studious	c. honest
4. quiet	d. sporty
5. dishonest	e. shy
6. hardworking	f. serious
7. unfriendly	g. friendly
8. funny	h. talkative

Grammar Skills

Interrogative Pronoun

The pronoun which asks a question is known as an **interrogative** pronoun.

Wh-words like **who**, **whom**, **whose**, **which**, **what**, etc., are used as interrogative pronouns to ask questions.

For example:

- **Which** of these colours is your favourite?
- **Who** asked for an ice-cream?
- **Whom** do you wish to meet?

E. Given below are some sentences. Form a question from each using an interrogative pronoun.

1. My pencil is red in colour. (what)

   ____

2. Arthur is responsible for the fault. (who)

   ____

3. Donna has placed her English book on the table. (where)

   ____

4. These bags are mine. (whose)

____

5. Our team won the game yesterday. (who)

____

6. City Hospital is the biggest building in this area. (which)

____

7. She wants coffee. (what)

____

8. He told Mary about this. (who)

____

Let us Know More

Helping others is the greatest quality of a human being. It costs nothing but the person who receives it, gets everything. Help is a word that implies assistance in doing certain kind of work. It can include several factors such as financial, mental, physical help, etc. No matter what kind of help you offer, no matter whom you help, it is more important to notice that another person is gaining something just because of your help. Helping others gives pleasure. However, everyone is busy and no one has enough time to help others. It is our responsibility to help people who are truly in need of assistance without expecting something in return. Help of any kind always gets counted. Helping others is like helping ourselves.

Fun Chat

Ma'am : Children, it is always nice to be helpful to the people in distress.

Child : But ma'am, why do you forget this at the time of exams? You never be nice to us and never let us be nice to others at that time.

10 Politeness

William was a young man who was **ill-tempered** and **ill-mannered**. When somebody gave him gifts, he would complain that it wasn't nice. Instead of saying 'thank you', he would hurt him/her by saying **harsh** words. If somebody had any problem, he made fun of him/her.

William had a good friend named Daniel, who was very polite. He used to speak gently with everybody. He didn't hurt anyone intentionally. When he got angry, he did not shout at others. Instead, he kept quiet. He tried to be soft-spoken and good to everyone.

One day, William and Daniel decided to go for a musical **concert**. Their favourite musician was performing at the concert. There was a huge rush for tickets. They both wanted to leave early to buy the tickets. However, they were caught up in the middle of heavy traffic. When they reached the ticket counter, just five minutes was left for the counter to close.

William went up to the counter and demanded in a rude manner, "Give us two tickets." The man at the counter was **shocked** at William's rudeness. He said, "The counter is closing. I am sorry; I cannot give you any ticket."

William started shouting again. Then, Daniel stopped him and went up to the counter.

Daniel smiled at the person at the counter and gently requested, "Hello sir! There is still two minutes left for the counter to be closed. Would you be kind enough to give us two tickets? We have come from a far-away place and we really want to attend the concert."

Daniel added, "I am very sorry for my friend's behaviour." The man at the ticket counter **obliged** Daniel with two tickets and closed the counter.

William was surprised to see this. He understood that whenever he was rude to people, he hurt them. It caused wounds in their hearts.

Daniel told William, "When you are good to others, they are good to you too. I would be happy if you learn good manners and be polite."

William and Daniel went to see the concert happily.

Know These Words

ill-tempered	-	getting angry easily
ill-mannered	-	rude and unpleasant
harsh	-	cruel
concert	-	a musical performance given in public
shocked	-	surprised
obliged	-	did someone a favour

Questions-Answers

A. Underline the correct answer.

1. What should we say when someone gives us gifts?

   a. Thank you b. Sorry c. It's not nice

2. Where did William and Daniel decide to go one day?

   a. Circus b. Musical concert c. Comedy show

3. What happens when we speak harsh words to others?

   a. It makes others happy

   b. It makes others rude

   c. It causes wounds in their hearts

B. Answer the following questions.

1. What kind of person was William?

____

____

2. What did he do when somebody gave him gifts?

____

____

3. Why was the man at the counter shocked and what did he say?

____

____

4. How did Daniel get tickets for the concert?

____

____

5. How was Daniel's behaviour with the man?

____

____

6. What did William understand?

____

____

Creative Writing

C. Are you often rude to others? Is it good to be rude to anyone?

____

____

D. How can our behaviour help us win the hearts of people around us?

Word Power

E. **Write two** synonyms **for each of the following.**

1. opponent
2. wit
3. mystify
4. dogged
5. wander
6. speak
7. present

Grammar Skills

Reflexive Pronouns

The pronoun that reflects the action done by the subject upon itself is called a reflexive pronoun. It is formed by adding **-self** (for singular number) or **-selves** (for plural number) to the personal pronoun. **Myself**, **herself**, **himself**, **itself**, **ourselves**, **themselves** are reflexive pronouns.

For example:

I painted the picture **myself**.

They pushed **themselves** in the crowd.

F. Write the antonym for each of the following adjectives.

	Antonym
1. sharp	____________
2. boring	____________
3. joyful	____________
4. wealthy	____________
5. kind	____________
6. trustworthy	____________
7. selfish	____________
8. disappointment	____________

G. Fill in the blanks with the appropriate reflexive pronouns.

1. She baked the cookies ________________ for the party.
2. He is completing the project ________________.
3. Emma has started walking ________________ without any support.
4. People parked their cars ________________ after looking at the sign.
5. The doctor attended his patients ________________.
6. I have hurt ________________.
7. The door of the house was closed ________________.
8. A five-year-old boy made a picture of her mother ________________.

Let us Know More

Politeness is a way of being polite to ourselves as well as to others. A polite child is a child who says and does everything in a polite and pleasing manner. Everybody loves those people who are respectful, helpful and polite. Among all good manners, politeness is the most important since everyone loves to hear something good and respectful. The persons who behave politely have already made themselves and their life precious. But, the persons who show rude and disobedient behaviour towards others gradually spoil their life. There are some magic words which really reflect politeness in our behaviour. Some of them are, **'sorry'**, **'excuse me'**, **'thank you'** and **'please'**.

Fun Chat

Do you know?

- If you burp after a meal, no need to say "excuse me" in China. It's a way of telling the chef that the meal was delicious.
- It is rude to smile at a stranger in Korea. It means you think he is foolish.
- In Russia, whistling indoors is considered rude; some think that doing so will bring bad luck.

11 Dreams

Images of hope,
Locked up fear you share,
Love and desire,
All in your head somewhere.

Dreams are wishes,
That let your **imagination** grow.
They let you travel,
Anywhere you can go.

Dreams show your happiest moments,
And what you **dread** in your heart.
They show you love, how to hold it,
And tell you where to start.

You could feel the beach,
The sand at your feet,
The heart and soul you'll be able to reach.

Words and images **swirl** in your mind,
That let you express yourself for all the times.

And when horrors are received,
And I fall on my knees,
Everything is **softened** by the **memories**,
the dreams.

Know These Words

locked up	-	closed something in a place or container
imagination	-	the ability of the mind to be thoughtful
dread	-	fear
swirl	-	to move in a twisting manner
softened	-	made something soft
memories	-	something remembered from the past

Questions-Answers

A. Underline the correct answer.

1. We have ___________ of hope in our mind.
2. Dreams let our ___________ grow.
3. We can feel ___________ at our feet in our dreams.
4. We get afraid when we see ___________ in our dream.

B. Answer the following questions.

1. What images are locked up in our head?

____

____

2. What are dreams?

____

____

3. What do dreams show us?

____

____

4. What let us express ourselves for all the time?

____

____

5. How is everything softened?

6. Find two abstract nouns from the poem.

7. What is the superlative degree of happy?

8. When did the poet fall on his knees?

9. Where are we able to reach in our dreams?

Creative Writing

C. Do you also dream at night? Is there any dream of you that has come true?

D. What is your dream for your future?

Word Power

E. Find the given words (in the Word Bank) in the word search.

o	p	a	i	m	u	r	a	y	j	s	o
e	r	z	r	u	p	s	e	d	k	d	p
l	e	d	t	i	y	p	c	r	k	s	l
q	p	e	u	t	z	o	d	e	z	d	t
t	a	y	c	r	x	l	r	a	s	t	y
y	r	u	u	i	c	u	s	m	t	t	r
z	e	e	p	e	v	y	d	i	i	p	p
u	y	r	o	d	r	t	r	e	u	i	l
z	a	c	h	i	e	v	e	v	o	g	a
r	t	e	v	e	r	y	o	n	e	h	n
i	n	s	p	i	r	i	n	g	p	j	r

Word Bank

aim plan achieve dream
tried inspiring prepare everyone

Grammar Skills

Determiners

The words **a, an** and **the** are determiners.

Definite Determiner and Indefinite Determiners

- **A** and **an** are **indefinite determiners.**
- **The** is called the **definite determiner.**

Indefinite Determiners

A and **an** are placed before **countable nouns** in the singular number.

Use of 'a'

Whenever a word begins with a consonant sound, we use '**a**' before it.

For example:

1. My neighbour is **a** doctor.
2. Puffy is **a** dog.

For vowels like **a**, **e**, **i**, **o**, **u**, if words start with them but make a **consonant sound**, we will use the article '**a**' only.

For example:

I have **a** one-hundred rupee note.

Use of 'an'

Whenever a word begins with a vowel sound, we use **an** before it.

For example: I read **an** interesting novel.

Even if a word starts with a consonant but makes a vowel sound, we use **an** before it.

For example:

an honest man ('ho' is pronounced as 'o', a vowel sound.)

F. Choose the correct indefinite determiner in each sentence.

1. I bought (a/an) pair of shoes.
2. I saw (a/an) movie last night.
3. Amy is (a/an) Spanish.
4. My brother does not eat (a/an) apple.
5. She read (a/an) amazing story yesterday.
6. This is (a/an) unique coin.
7. Please wait for (a/an) hour for the test results.
8. Richard is (a/an) MBA from Cambridge University.
9. Noah is wearing (a/an) blue shirt.
10. I saw (a/an) one-eyed man.

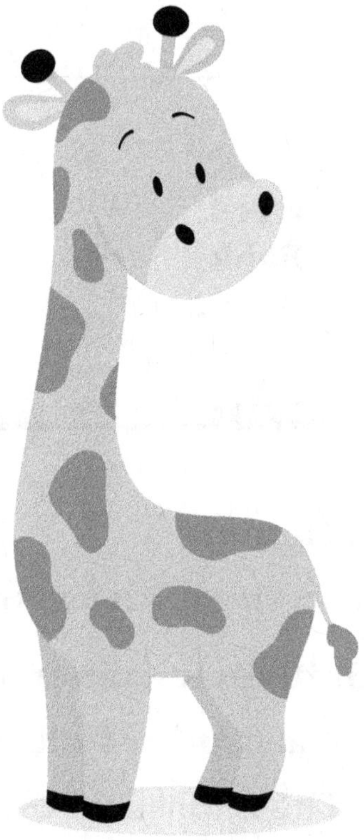

Let us Know More

Dreams are stories and images our mind creates while we are asleep. Dreams can be vivid. They can make you feel happy, sad or scared. Sometimes they may seem confusing or irrational.

Dreams can occur anytime during sleep. But the most vivid dreams occur during deep REM (rapid eye movement) sleep, when the brain remains most active.

Fun Chat

Read the joke and laugh aloud.

Teacher : John, today you are late again.

John : Teacher, I was just dreaming that I was playing football.

And my game went late because of heavy rain in the playground.

☺ ☺ ☺

12 Value of Good Health

Good health is a **boon**. It is the most precious **possession** of man. If man loses his health, he loses all the **charms** of the world. Ask the man who has lost his health; he can tell you the value of good health. Health is the real wealth of a man.

A sound mind in a sound body is an old saying. Healthy minds can be found only in healthy bodies. Sick men have sick minds. Their attitude towards life is **gloomy**. On the other hand, if man has good health, his outlook towards life is also healthy. He can work for long hours without feeling tired. If a student has good health, his memory will be good and his mind will be sharp. There are certain things which are essential for good health. Nutritious food comes first. Fresh air is also important for good health. People living in the open air usually enjoy good health. Exercise plays a great role in making man healthy.

There are certain things which are bad for health. We should guard ourselves against them. Smoking is **injurious** to health. Eating too much spoils one's digestive system. If a man is irregular in his habits, he is likely to lose his health.

Know These Words

boon	-	a thing that is helpful
possession	-	the state of having something
charms	-	attractions
gloomy	-	dark
injurious	-	harmful

Questions-Answers

A. Underline the correct answer.

1. What is the real wealth of a man?

   a. Money   b. Jewellery   c. Health

2. ______________ is injurious to health.

   a. Smoking   b. Drinking   c. Exercising

3. Eating too much ______________ one's digestive system.

   a. spoils   b. improves   c. creates

4. What thing is the most essential for good health?

   a. Nutritious food   b. Fresh air   c. Exercise

B. Answer the following questions.

1. What is good health?

   ____

   ____

2. Who can tell the value of good health?

   ____

   ____

3. Where can the healthy minds be found?

   ____

   ____

4. Who has healthy outlook towards life?

____

____

5. What type of food should we eat for good health?

____

____

Creative Writing

C. What type of food do you eat? Does it keep you healthy?

____

____

____

____

____

____

D. How can you say that a healthy mind resides in a healthy body?

____

____

____

____

____

____

Word Power

E. Write a single word for each of the following:

1. A food-item that is used with other food-items in the preparation of a particular dish. ______________
2. Eating more than your body needs. ______________

3. Someone eats less food, or only particular types of food because he/she wants to become thinner or does so for medical reason. ____________________

4. Any of a group of natural substances which are necessary in small amounts for the growth and good health of the body. ____________________

5. Extremely fat ____________________

Grammar Skills

Adjectives

Adjectives are describing words that tell us more about nouns or pronouns.

For example:

She has very **long** hair.

Adjective of Quality

An adjective of quality is an adjective showing the quality of a noun or pronoun.

We must remember to ask the question '**What kind of?**' in case of adjective of quality.

For example:

Noah plays in a **big** ground.

F. Fill in the blanks with the adjectives of quality.

1. The rhinoceros is a __________ animal.
2. The child wore a __________ dress.
3. She had __________ hair.
4. The young man drove a __________ car.
5. The old lady lived in a __________ house.
6. Daisy is a __________ student.
7. Uncle Adam wore a __________ cap.
8. Mrs Katherine has a __________ basket in her hand.

Let us Know More

Laughing is good for the heart and can increase blood flow by 20 per cent.

Your skin works hard. Not only is it the largest organ in the body but it also defends against disease and infections, regulates your temperature and aids in vitamin production.

Always look on the bright side; being an optimist can help you live longer.

Fun Chat

Read the jokes and laugh aloud.

Doctor : You should take at least 10 glasses of water every day.

Patient : It is impossible.

Doctor : Why?

Patient : I have only 4 glasses at home.

A man goes to the doctor with big bandages over both ears.

"What happened to your ears?" the doctor asks.

"I was ironing my shirt and the phone rang," the man says.

"And what happened to the other ear?"

"Just as I put the iron down," the phone rang again.

13 Obedience

Once there lived a little boy named Jacob. He had a younger sister named Elie. They went to school together. They also played together in the evening.

Jacob was a very **obedient** boy. He used to teach his sister to be obedient but she did not listen to him.

One day, Jacob's mother decided to take her children to a fair. That fair had swings, giant wheels and other joy rides. The fair also had stalls of candies, soft drinks and ice creams. There were also stalls for children's books and toys. Jacob and Elie were very **excited** to see all this.

Mom told the children, "Do not leave my hand in the fair. Many children do not listen to their parents and get lost in the fair. The fair is huge and very **crowded**. Anybody can get lost."

Jacob carefully heard what mother said to him. But Elie took no notice of it.

On a bright Sunday morning, Jacob, Elie and their mother left for the fair. At the fair, they took many rides. They also ate ice cream and candies.

It was almost time to

leave. All of a sudden, Mom realised that Elie was missing. Mom got **worried**. She told Jacob, "Keep standing right here till I come. Don't move till I find Elie and come back."

Jacob was an obedient child. He kept waiting. It was getting dark. People were leaving the fair to go back home. Jacob's neighbours had also come to the fair. Finding him standing alone, they called out, "Come quickly. It is getting dark."

Jacob waved them saying, "My mother asked me to stand here. She knows what is best for me."

Jacob's mother found Elie at a candy shop far away. She was standing there and crying. On seeing her mother, she exclaimed with sorrow, "Sorry Mom! I will always be obedient from now."

Mother called for a taxi and came to pick up Jacob. Small but brave, Jacob was standing at the same place. The mother's heart was filled with love for her obedient son.

Know These Words

obedient	-	respectful
excited	-	feeling very happy
crowded	-	full of people
worried	-	concerned

Questions-Answers

A. Underline the correct answer.

1. What is the name of the boy in the story?

   a. Elie b. Jacob c. Max

2. What is the name of the girl in the story?

   a. Elie b. Jacob c. Sophia

3. What kind of boy was Jacob?

   a. Sincere b. Liar c. Obedient

4. Who asked Jacob to come quickly?

   a. Mom b. Neighbours c. Elie

B. Answer the following questions.

1. What did Jacob always teach to her sister?

2. What kind of stalls did the fair have?

3. Where did mom, Jacob and Elie go on one Sunday morning?

4. Why did mom get worried?

5. Who was Jacob waiting for in the fair when it was getting dark?

6. Where did Jacob's mom find Elie?

7. What did Elie say on seeing her mom?

Creative Writing

C. Do you always obey your parents and elders? How is obeying our elders helpful to us?

____

____

____

____

____

____

____

D. Have you visited a fair? How did you enjoy there?

____

____

____

____

____

____

Word Power

E. Replace each highlighted word with its antonym**.**

1. I couldn't stay **asleep** ________________ during the movie.
2. The plane will **leave** ________________ at four in the afternoon.
3. I ate my ice cream the **slowest** ________________.
4. Henry collected the **least** ________________ of the seashells.
5. I am **disappointed** ________________; we won our first soccer game.
6. The leopard is a **tame** ________________ animal.
7. My dad helped me **break** ________________ my favourite toy boat.
8. She is extremely **reckless** ________________ when she drives.

9. Sophia doesn't like to swim in the **shallow** ________________ end.

10. This pillow is **hard** ________________ and fluffy.

Grammar Skills

Determiners of Quantity

A determiner of quantity tells us about the quantity of a thing. It answers the question, '**how much**?'

For example:

1. There is **some** water in the pot.
2. We do not have **enough** time.

Determiners of Number

A determiner of number expresses the number of persons or things. It answers the question, '**how many**'.

The **fourth** boy is the monitor.

There are **no** pictures in the book.

Determiners of number are of three kinds:

Definite numeral determiners, which denote an exact number, as;

Cardinals :	one	two	three
Ordinals :	first	second	third

Indefinite numeral determiners, which do not denote an exact number, as;

all	no	many	few
some	any	certain	several

Distributive numeral determiners, which refer to each one of a number, as

each	every

F. Tick (✓) either the determiner of quantity or the determiner of number.

1. Zoya goes to her tutorial class (each/five) days a week.
2. I have invited (few/less) people to my family function.
3. How (much/many) rings does she wear?
4. There are (much/many) schools in our city.

5. There are (few/little) cars on the road at weekends.
6. If you do (all/little) homework today, you will have very (few/less) homework to do tomorrow.
7. We do not have (some/enough) money to buy that dispenser.
8. (Each/Every) boy must take his turn.

Let us Know More

We should follow these instructions to be obedient.

1. Commit yourself and decide to be obedient towards worthy, righteous and reasonable rules.
2. Listen to your elders when they ask you to do something because they are more experienced than you.
3. Start asking yourself how obeying that rule is going to benefit you in life.
4. Be humble and grateful so that it may help you become less rebellious and more obedient.

Fun Chat

Read the joke and laugh aloud.

Rich man : Michael (the butler), for 30 years you have been bringing me coffee, filled to the brim, without even spilling a drop. How do you manage that over these stairs?

Michael : Sir, before I climb up the stairs I take a big sip; as I get upstairs, I put it back.

Unfortunately, that was the last day of the butler.

☺ ☺ ☺

14 The True Meaning of Life

The years have passed by,
In the **blink** of an eye,
Moments of sadness,
And joy have flown by.

People I loved,
Have come and have gone,
But the world never stopped,
And we all carried on.

Life wasn't easy,
And the **struggles** were there,
Filled with times that it mattered,
Times I just didn't care.

I stood on my own,
And I still found my way,
Through some nights filled with tears,
And the **dawn** of new days.

And now with old age,
It's become very clear,
Things I once found important,
Were not why I was here.

And how many things,
That I managed to buy,
Were never what made me,
Feel better inside.

And the worries and fears,
That **plagued** me each day,
In the end of it all,
Would just fade away.

But how much I reached out,
To others when needed,
Would be the true measure,
Of how I succeeded.

And how much I shared,
Of my soul and my heart,
Would ultimately be,
What set me apart.

And what's really important,
Is my opinion of me,
And whether or not,
I'm the best I can be.

And how much more **kindness**,
And love I can show,
Before the Lord tells me,
It's my time to go.

Know These Words

blink	-	shutting and opening the eyes quickly
struggle	-	tussle; problem
dawn	-	start of a new day
plagued	-	troubled
kindness	-	mercy; quality of being friendly

Questions-Answers

A. Fill in the blanks.

1. __________ have passed very quickly.
2. The __________ of sadness and joy have flown by.
3. The __________ never stops even when the people come and go from our life.
4. We should be __________ in our own opinion.
5. We should show our __________ to everyone throughout our life.

B. Answer the following questions.

1. At what stage of life is the poet writing this poem?

   ____

2. What does the poet mean by saying 'But the world never stopped'?

   ____

3. Was the poet's life easy? What did he have to face in his life?

   ____

4. What were the nights filled with?

   ____

5. What did the poet find in his old age?

   ____

6. What is really important according to the poet?

   ____

7. What is the true measure of success?

   ____

8. Choose the word that means 'distressed'.

   ____

9. Find a word that is used both as a noun and a pronoun. It is also used as an adjective.

   ____

Creative Writing

C. Success isn't about how much money you make; it's about the difference you make in other people's life.

Write your views to justify the statement.

____

____

____

____

D. What is the most important thing to live a beautiful life?

____

____

____

Word Power

E. Find the words in the word grid.

a	t	r	h	o	n	e	s	t	y	u	i	c	o	y	p
t	s	e	u	q	u	r	q	e	t	i	p	o	t	k	e
y	y	s	i	r	i	t	e	s	y	o	y	u	y	o	r
e	z	p	t	c	a	r	i	n	g	p	t	r	l	p	s
z	r	e	i	t	o	y	e	e	u	z	v	a	k	t	e
t	y	c	i	i	p	j	i	o	i	x	c	g	s	i	v
i	u	t	o	p	s	d	t	y	u	z	d	e	a	v	e
t	r	u	s	t	w	o	r	t	h	i	n	e	s	s	r
u	z	e	y	u	i	p	z	x	v	n	j	k	l	p	a
r	e	s	p	o	n	s	i	b	i	l	i	t	y	i	n
u	c	i	t	i	z	e	n	s	h	i	p	t	b	o	c
f	a	i	r	n	e	s	s	y	y	u	o	p	z	x	e
t	u	u	f	r	i	e	n	d	s	h	i	p	t	z	b

Word Bank			
respect	caring	fairness	responsibility
honesty	courage	friendship	perseverance
citizenship	trustworthiness		

Grammar Skills

Demonstrative Determiners

A demonstrative determiner points out a particular person/thing.

It answers the question, **which one**?

This, that, these and **those** are demonstrative determiners. These can also be used as **demonstrative pronouns**.

For example:

1. **This** shirt is Edwin's.
2. Look! Uncle Robert lives in **that** house.

Demonstrative Determiner	Demonstrative Pronoun
This pen belongs to Cindy.	**This** is Cindy's pen.
I have seen **that** episode.	**That** is the episode I have seen.

F. Make two sentences using each given word as a demonstrative determiner and as a demonstrative pronoun.

1. This ______________________________

   ____

2. That ______________________________

   ____

3. Those ______________________________

   ____

4. These ______________________________

   ____

G. Tick (✓) the correct options from the brackets.

1. (This/These) college campus is vast.
2. I have read (this/those) books.
3. My book is lying on (that/those) table.
4. Does (this/these) smell weird?
5. Who brought (this/these) crackers?
6. Many states of (this/those) country are prosperous.
7. Justin wants (these/that) pen.

Let us Know More

Helping others should be the motive of everyone's life. The most important rule of helping people should be to find what's actually valuable to someone. The second important rule is taking out time. Time is valuable and most people understand that. When you take time out of your day to help a friend, he/she remembers it. The third rule is giving gifts. Giving gifts is very tricky since we want to give our friends gifts that make sense and help them.

Fun Chat

Read the joke and laugh aloud.

First Student	:	Can you see God?
Second Student	:	No.
First Student	:	Can you touch God?
Second Student	:	No.
First Student	:	Then there isn't any God.
Second Student	:	Can you see your brain?
First Student	:	No.
Second Student	:	Can you touch your brain?
First Student	:	No.
Second Student	:	Okay, so you don't have a brain.

☺ ☺ ☺

15 Admitting Our Faults

There is a famous proverb — To err is human. Err means making a mistake. Mistakes make man perfect. They help us master the subject. It is through our mistakes that we learn and achieve success. No person in this world, be it a scientist, poet, creative painter or the world's best sportsman, can shine without committing any mistake.

Mistakes and failures are the **foundations** of a strong and bright future. As we know, failures are the **pillars** of success; we must always learn from our mistakes. The most difficult virtue to gain on the earth is to admit our own faults. If we are **courageous** enough to admit our mistakes, then we will be able to overcome our shortcomings. History is the record of our past experiences. It enriches us with the knowledge to overcome the mistakes that we had committed in the past.

David had great interest in painting. He had beautifully painted birds, mountains and animals on paper. He had worked hard to learn the art of drawing. He had earned prizes for his drawings.

Once, he participated in a Drawing Competition where he was allowed to sketch on a board with paint and brushes. His painting was not appreciated. It was not even selected in the top ten paintings. He became so **impatient** that he started to **blame** the organizers. Gradually, he realised his fault and decided to practise more through hard work. His effort yielded him the fruit of success. He succeeded in winning the first prize.

We should never feel ashamed in admitting our own mistakes. We should always try to learn from our faults.

Know These Words

foundation(s)	-	basis
pillars	-	support
courageous	-	fearless
impatient	-	restless
blame	-	to hold someone responsible for a wrong act

Questions-Answers

A. Underline the correct answer.

1. __________ make man perfect.

   a. Success b. Mistakes c. Practice

2. What are the pillars of success?

   a. Mistakes b. Organizers c. Failures

B. Answer the following questions.

1. What are mistakes and failures?

   ____

   ____

2. How are failures the pillars of success?

   ____

   ____

3. What is the most difficult virtue to gain on the earth?

4. How does history help us?

5. What had David beautifully painted?

6. What did David do after realising his fault?

7. What did it yield after years of practice?

8. What do we learn from this story?

Creative Writing

C. Do you make mistakes at the workplace? Do you try to correct them?

D. How do you behave when you realise your mistake?

Word Power

E. Make five pairs of words with similar meanings.

Word Bank					
	hurt	loyal	large	sleepy	serious
	huge	grave	injure	drowsy	faithful

a. ______ ______ b. ______ ______ c. ______ ______

d. ______ ______ e. ______ ______

Grammar Skills

Adverb

The word that tells the quality of a verb, where it is done and when it is done, is called an **adverb**.

For example:

The sun shines **brightly**.

They **seldom** go to the cinema.

Adverbs of Time

The word that indicates the time of action and answers the question, '**when**', is called an adverb of time.

For example : early, soon, late, yet, still, already, recently, today, etc.

1. He is **still** sleeping.
2. He wakes up **early** in the morning.

F. Complete the following story using the adverbs given in the box.

already	yet	late	early	today	luckily	quickly

Usually, I get up (1) ______________ in the morning. But, (2) ______________ I got up at 7 o'clock. I was (3) ______________ for school. My school bus arrives at 7:30 am. I had no chance to board it.

(4)_____________Ihadnotlosthope.I(5)_____________tookmybath.Myschooluniformwas (6) _____________ ironed. I wore it, took my school bag and rushed towards the bus stop. (7) _____________, the bus was (8) _____________. I didn't miss it. I promised myself to always remember the nursery rhyme. '(9) _____________ to bed, (10) _____________ to rise, makes a man healthy, wealthy and wise.

Let us Know More

Life is a struggle. It is a mixture of successes and failures. Nobody can be sure of success throughout his life. Failure can come in any venture and that too sometimes unexpectedly. A person, who loses heart after failure, is a lost soul. But a person who takes failure in its own stride and continues his efforts for success, does succeed in the long run. It is rightly said that failures are the stepping stones to success. They may seem worthless in their own way but they have their essential value.

Fun Chat

Father : Why did you get such a low score in that exam? Were you absent on the day of the exam?

Son : No. But the boy who sits next to me was absent.

☺ ☺ ☺

Son : Why has some of your hair gone white, dad?

Father : Every time a son makes his dad unhappy, one of his father's hair turns white.

Son : *(Innocently)* Now I understand why grandpa has got all his hair white.

16 Advantages of the Cinema

One of the most wonderful gifts of science is the cinema. It has become the most popular source of recreation. The importance of the cinema is felt in every sphere of life, such as education, social, political and moral.

The cinema provides a cheap form of entertainment to people.It takes us away from the hard realities of life. It entertains us with interesting stories, melodious songs and **enchanting** dances. Town life is incomplete without the cinema.

The cinema is a great source of information as well. We may not be able to visit all the parts of our country and some countries, but we can learn a lot about them through films. The news reels and the documentary films make our knowledge up to date about recent developments. We see a picture about New York or Washington, we see the pictures of American **skyscrapers**, how the people move there in streets, how they dress up and their ways of doing particular tasks. No book on geography could give us the clear idea or picture about all these things.

We can also make the best use of the cinema or films in **imparting** education to students. Almost all the school subjects can easily be taught through films. Geography can nicely be taught by showing the **illustrations** of different landscapes, mountains, rivers, waterfalls, springs and different regions in movies. Experiments in science can also be shown on the screen. A film can also serve the purpose of the medium of teaching civics. Likewise, other subjects can also be taught through films.

The cinema helps build a nation as well. In countries, where the masses are illiterate and cannot benefit from books and papers, the cinema can be a great source for their knowledge. Films can teach civics and hygiene to the masses. They could make the people aware of keeping their streets and cities clean, fighting against diseases and living a happy life. The cinema can also teach people how to talk, walk and dress well.

Know These Words

enchanting	-	alluring
skyscrapers	-	very tall buildings
imparting	-	sharing something, especially knowledge
illustrations	-	examples used for clarifying something

Questions-Answers

A. Underline the correct answer.

1. What has become the most popular source of recreation?

   a. Cinema b. Circus shows c. Travelling

2. The cinema provides a _______ form of entertainment to people.

   a. costly b. cheap c. good

3. Which subject performs experiments?

   a. English b. Geography c. Science

4. What life is incomplete without a cinema?

   a. Town b. Village c. School

5. The cinema is a great source of _______________.

   a. information b. data c. knowledge

B. Answer the following questions.

1. In what spheres of life the importance of the cinema is felt?

2. How does the cinema entertain us?

3. What can we learn from films?

4. What ideas cannot be given by any book?

5. How can we make the best use of the cinema?

6. How can geography be nicely taught?

7. How can films make people aware?

Creative Writing

C. What information do you get from the cinema?

____

____

____

____

____

____

____

D. Do you think the cinema has only advantages? Can you state any one disadvantage of the cinema?

____

____

____

____

____

____

____

Word Power

E. Write an appropriate word for each sentence.

1. Something written by hand for making a good movie is called a ________________.
2. A performer in a theatre, television, or film is called an ________________.
3. A series of moving pictures that tells a story is called a ________________.
4. Someone who finances and supervises the making of a show is called a ________________.
5. A photographer who operates a camera for television or film making ________________.
6. The office where tickets of admission are sold is called ________________.

Grammar Skills

Adverbs of Place

The adverb that indicates the place of action and answers the question, '**where**', is called the **adverb of place**. Some commonly used adverbs of place are **here**, **there**, **near**, **up**, **down**, **in**, **out**, **everywhere**, **somewhere**, **nowhere**, etc.

For example:

Lucy ran **upstairs** to her bedroom.

F. Read the following sentences. Underline the adverbs of place in them. Make new sentences using the same adverbs. Follow the example.

The meeting will be held here.

Here : You can sit here.

1. Sharon is sleeping upstairs.

____

____

2. Go downstairs.

____

____

3. Come near and take this book.

____

____

4. Where there is a will, there is a way.

____

____

5. God is everywhere.

____

____

6. He has gone out.

____

____

Let us Know More

The cinema is one of the most important inventions of modern science. This invention was made by Thomas Edison, a famous American scientist. The cinema is an effective medium for education and recreation as well. It plays a crucial role in social, political, educational and moral life. It has come to occupy an important place in our life. It has many advantages and disadvantages. If the right types of films with social and moral messages are produced, they can bring about the much needed reforms and changes to our society. If films are not produced sensibly, it can deflect the minds of the audience.

Fun Chat

Guess the names of these Hollywood movies for the dialogues given below:

1. "I'm gonna make him an offer he can't refuse."
2. "They may take our lives, but they will never take... our freedom!"
3. "You can't handle the truth!"

Choose your answers from here:

Brave Heart Few Good Men The Godfather

17 Trust

Friendship knows no bounds. We can trust a friend who never proves to be ungrateful and **treacherous**. Love and respect are the foundations of a true friendship. Trust is the centre around which all relationships revolve.

Once, there lived a king who was loved and respected by his people. He had a team of efficient ministers who assisted him in all the important matters of decision-making. The king had a great interest of hunting wild animals. He used to drive his **chariot** towards the forest where he enjoyed hunting.

One day, the king went into the jungle for hunting a deer. He drove the chariot deep into the jungle. The king ran miles into the wood but failed to hunt any deer.

The disappointed king decided to return to the palace. He suddenly heard the roar of a lion which was approaching towards him. The roar was so loud and sudden that the king threw the bow and arrows on the ground. The king started running to save his life from the **mighty** lion. In a flash, he climbed up a tree to escape the lion. As he stared at the lion with a breath of relief, the unfortunate king found that a bear was sitting on the top of the same tree. Out of fear, the king began to sweat.

His life was hanging between the lion and the bear. The bear understood that the king was frightened. He politely said, "Don't be scared, O King! I will not harm you. Trust me. I am sitting on the tree to save my life from this wild lion." The king, getting assurance from the bear, slept on the **lap** of the bear. Realising that the king had slept, the lion began to convince the bear and said, "Push the king down; I will have my dinner and walk back to the den."

The bear strongly refused the lion's proposal by saying that he could not kill the king, as the king had full faith in him.

The king, after enjoying a sound sleep, woke up. He thanked the bear for taking care of him while he was sleeping. Now, the lion asked the king to push the bear down from the tree. He would carry the bear to his den as his **cubs** were hungry and his wife was sick. But, the king refused to **comply** with the lion's order. The disheartened lion left the place. Trust kept the **dignity** of friendship between the king and the bear.

Know These Words

treacherous	-	unfaithful
chariot	-	a two-wheeled vehicle drawn by horses
mighty	-	powerful
lap	-	the flat area between the waist and knee of a seated person or animal.
cubs	-	the young ones of a lion
comply	-	to act according to an order
dignity	-	calm behaviour that makes people respect you

Questions-Answers

A. Underline the correct answer.

1. What is the centre around which all relationships revolve?

   a. Trust b. Gratefulness c. Respect

2. What great interest did the king have?

   a. hunting wild animals

   b. killing domestic animals

   c. taming wild animals

3. Whom did the lion try to convince first?

   a. King b. Bear c. Cubs

4. Love and _______ are the foundations of a true friendship.

   a. insult b. respect c. faith

B. Answer the following questions.

1. Who can we trust?

   ____

   ____

2. What did the king do to escape the lion?

   ____

   ____

3. What did the bear say to the king?

   ____

   ____

4. Who did the lion begin to convince after the king had slept?

   ____

   ____

5. What did the lion ask the king?

   ____

   ____

Creative Writing

C. Do you have a friend who you can trust completely and share your secrets with?

____

____

____

____

____

____

D. Are you a trustworthy friend? Justify it with the help of an example.

____

____

____

____

____

____

Word Power

E. Complete the crossword puzzle using the hints.

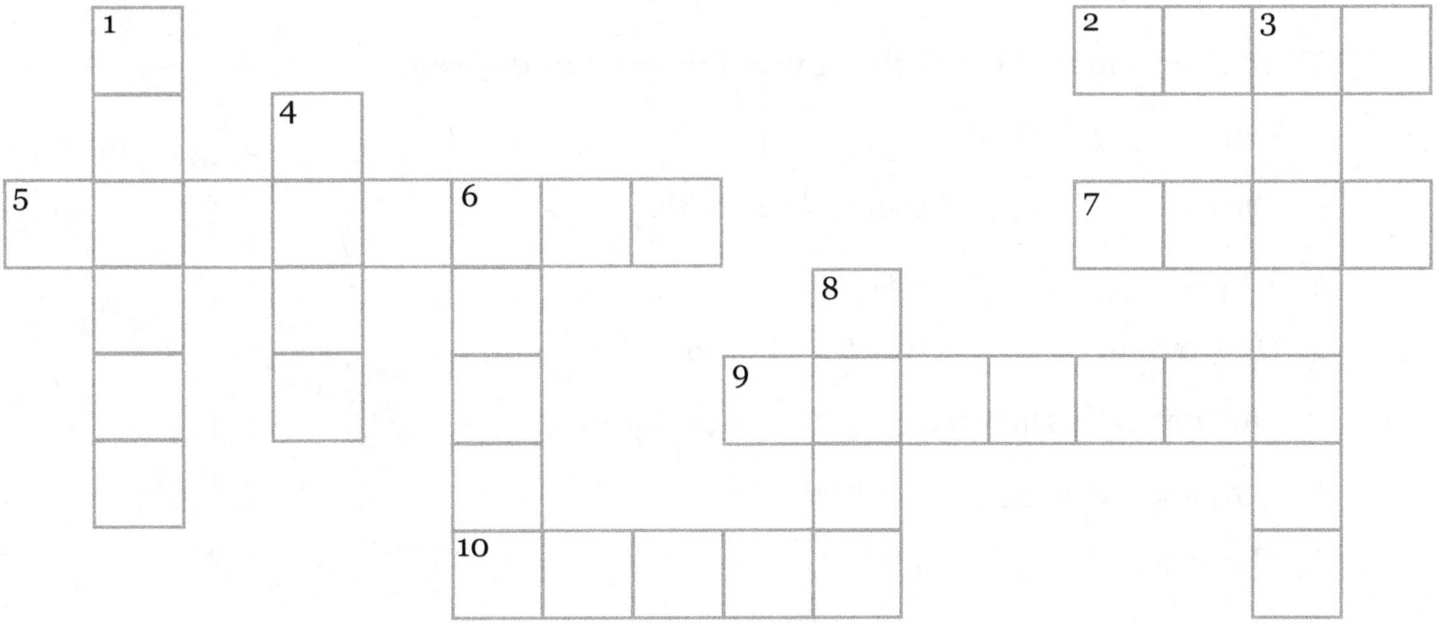

Across

2. Unwell
5. Having great strength
7. To perform songs with your voice
9. A time of difficulty or need
10. Enjoying pleasure, satisfaction or joy

Down

1. To pour oil on someone
3. To admit that you have sinned
4. To make a person well
6. Belief
8. To speak to or make a request to God

Word Bank				
trouble	sing	heal	confess	powerful
happy	pray	sick	faith	anoint

Grammar Skills

Adverbs of degree

The adverb that answers the question '**how much, to what extent**' is known as an **adverb of degree**. **Very**, **too**, **really**, **enough**, **just**, **quite**, **almost**, **fairly**, **rather**, etc., are adverbs of degree.

For example :

The coffee is **too** sweet.

The tea is **rather** hot.

F. Fill in the blanks with the suitable adverbs of degree.

1. I am ________ tired.
2. She has a ________ pleasing personality.
3. You are ________ careless.
4. Her voice is ________ sweet.
5. The rent of this house is ________ high for me.
6. Your answer is ________ different.
7. The glass is ________ full.

8. The food is ________ delicious.

9. He has done ________well.

10. Thank you ________ much.

Let us Know More

All relationships are based on trust. Children need to trust their parents. Parents need to trust their children. Trust makes honest communication possible. It builds relational bridges. It gives meaning to our respective roles. It provides security. It stimulates responsibility and caring. If a child doesn't learn to trust, the consequences can be calamitous. So, there must be a bond and trust between parents and a child. We should also remember that trust and understanding between two best friends is same as the ceiling of a house which holds the house. The the same way this relation holds two best friends together.

Fun Chat

Answer the given riddle.

What is that you ought to keep after you have given it to someone else?

18 Steadfast Heart

I've dreamed
many dreams
That never came true
I've seen them **vanish** at **dawn**,
But I've realised
Enough of my dreams,
Thank God,
To make me want to dream on.

I've prayed many prayers,
When no answer came,
Though I waited **patient** and long,
But answers have come,
To enough of my prayers,
Thank God,
To make me keep praying on.

I've trusted many a friend that failed,
And left me to **weep** alone,
But I've found
Many of my friends **true blue**,
Thank God,
To make me keep trusting on.

I've sown many seeds
That fell by the way,
For the birds to feed upon,
But I've held

Enough golden **sheaves** in my hands,
Thank God,
To make me keep sowing on.

I've **drained** the cup
Of disappointment and pain
And gone many ways without song,
But I've sipped enough **nectar**
From the roses of life
Thank God,
To make me want to live on.

Know These Words

vanish	-	to disappear
dawn	-	daybreak
patient	-	able to stay calm
weep	-	to cry, grieve
true blue	-	highly faithful
sheaves	-	grain stalks
drained	-	emptied out
nectar	-	a sweet liquid produced by flowers

Questions-Answers

A. Fill in the blanks with the suitable words.

1. The dreams we see mostly ________ at dawn.
2. We should never leave our friends to weep ________.
3. The birds feed upon the ________ seeds.
4. We should deflate ________ and ________ from our life.
5. We should ________ even the small things of life.

B. Answer the following questions.

1. Do we all remember our dreams?

2. What does the poet do when he does not get answer to many of his prayers?

3. What did many friends do to the poet?

4. What does the poet want to describe about enough of his friends?

5. What has the poet held in his hands?

6. What has the poet taken to make himself want to live on?

7. What lesson does the poem give us?

Creative Writing

C. What do you mean by optimism? What is the difference between an optimistic and a pessimistic person?

____

____

____

____

____

____

Word Power

D. Solve the crossword puzzle using the hints given on the next page.

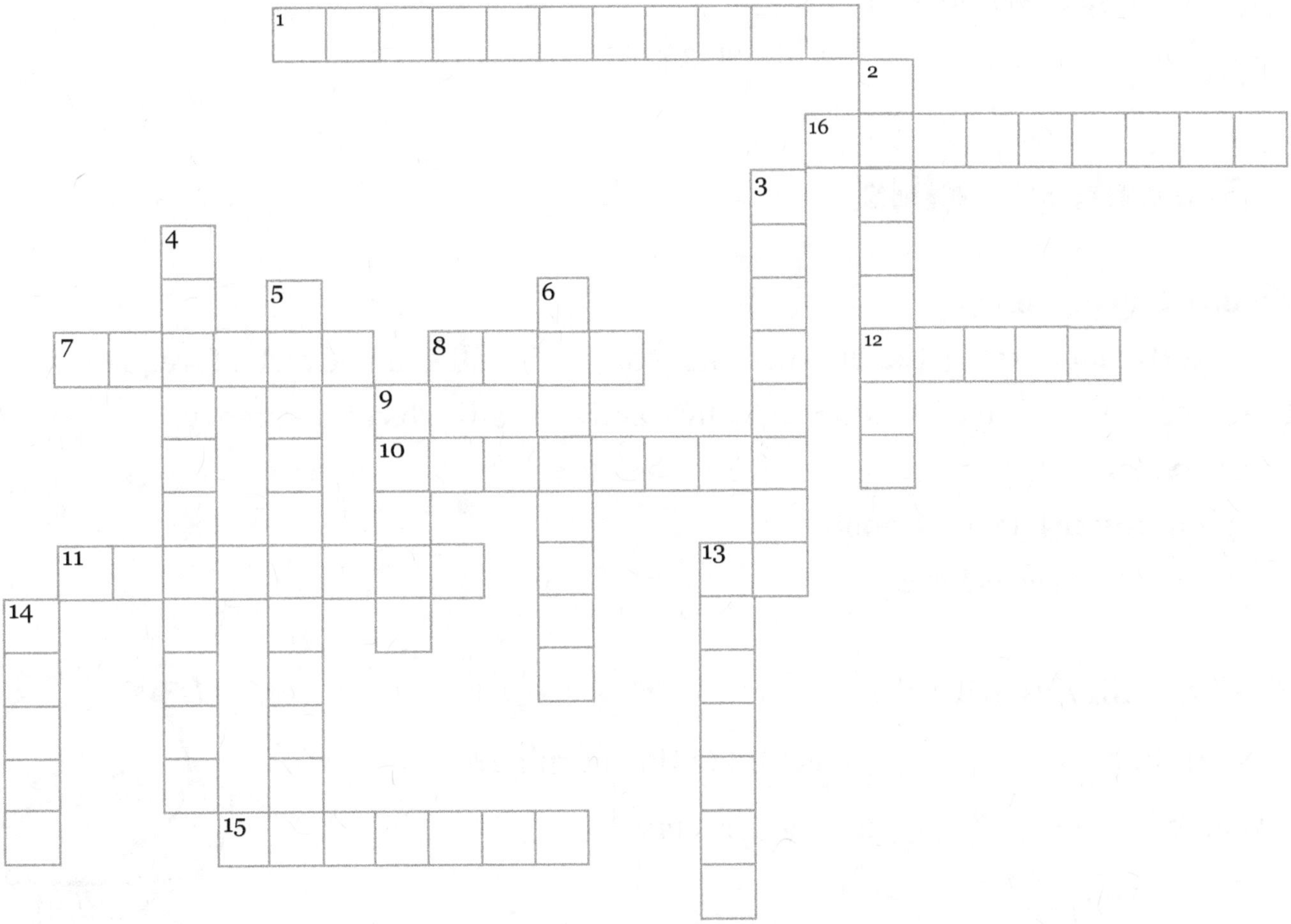

Across

1. Try giving __________ to others.
7. The __________ is good news.
8. Life is __________ when we enjoy small things too.
10. Develop an __________ of happiness.
11. __________ comes with repentance.
12. We must __________ God for letting us have the ride.
15. We should __________ in ourselves.
16. Disobedience never brings __________.

Down

2. Try to have much fun and __________ in life.
3. __________ do not achieve success.
4. Don't get __________ when you get criticism.
5. We are __________ for our own happiness.
6. Always look towards the __________ side.
9. We must replace our fears with our __________.
13. We must live the life to its __________.
14. We must __________ our blessings.

Grammar Skills

Adverbs of Frequency

The adverb that answers the question 'how often', is called an adverb of frequency. Never, always, sometimes, seldom, after, usually, rarely are adverbs of frequency.

For example:

I am **never** late for school.

He **seldom** goes here.

E. Fill in the blanks with the adverbs of frequency.

1. What time do you _________ get up in the morning?
2. Where do you _________ go after the class?
3. Who do you _________ talk to?
4. What do you _________ do on the weekend?

5. What do you ________ watch on TV?

6. Where do you ________ eat lunch?

Let us Know More

Being an optimist does not mean that you are out of touch with reality, ignoring difficulties and obstacles and behaving in an innocent way.

Being an optimist means that you hope and expect events and plan to turn out well, and that you look with a smile at the future.

It is important to be well poised, using common sense, not just telling yourself that nothing bad can ever happen to you and closing your eyes to the reality.

Doing so can lead to being impractical, taking bad decisions, and letting people ridicule or take advantage of you. An optimist sees both good and bad, but at the same time, expects success and puts forth efforts to make things turn out well.

We should adopt the attitude of optimism since it keeps us motivated and energetic. It helps us focus on our vision and makes everyday life a blessing.

Fun Chat

Read the joke and laugh aloud.

Two people were driving to Disneyland.

The sign board said–Disneyland left.

So, they started crying and headed home.

☺ ☺ ☺

Alex : What should one do when no one laughs at one's science jokes?

Sheldox : One should keep trying until one gets a reaction.

☺ ☺ ☺

19 Discipline Builds a Nation

Discipline is the process of training oneself in **obedience**, **self-control** and skill. The controlled and ordered behaviour results from such training. Discipline is the basis of the whole universe. The solar system is governed by certain laws to maintain perfect **harmony** and beauty. Without this order, there would be an utter **chaos**.

Discipline is a basic requirement of a civilized society. Citizens of a disciplined nation work with a spirit of cooperation and unity. Aristotle rightly said, "Discipline is obedience to rules formed by the society for the good of all."

Discipline should be inculcated from a very young age. Talent and genius alone are not enough to achieve success. Discipline has an equally important role to play. Talent blossoms in a disciplined person.

Discipline is not only desirable but also **indispensable**. Absence of discipline means decay. To prevent decay, discipline has to be imposed in the common interest and for the common good of all.

Discipline is important in the family. Parents must raise their children in a pleasant and disciplined atmosphere. They should teach them the right values. Children growing in disciplined and happy homes become responsible adults.

Discipline is the lifeline of the military departments. These armed forces follow a certain code of conduct. It demands loyalty to the country and to superior officers. It demands a spirit of fellowship and readiness to cope with an emergency. It is the duty of a soldier to obey the orders of his commander. No army can put up a brave front against the enemy if it lacks discipline.

People create chaos in public places by their undisciplined behaviour. They show lack of order and manners while boarding buses and trains. The rising crime graph in the country is due to the lack of discipline. So, it is true to say that discipline ensures justice and fair play.

Know These Words

obedience	-	the act of following the orders
self-control	-	the ability to control your emotions
harmony	-	orderly arrangement
chaos	-	a state of great disorder
indispensable	-	that cannot be neglected

Questions-Answers

A. Underline the correct answer.

1. What is the basis of the whole universe?

   a. Planets   b. Stars   c. Discipline

2. What blossoms in a disciplined person?

   a. Success   b. Talent   c. Genius

3. Parents should teach the children the right ________

   a. values   b. subjects   c. path

4. It is the duty of a _________ to obey the orders of his _________.
   a. commander, soldier
   b. soldier, commander
   c. teacher, students

5. How do people create chaos in public places?
   a. Due to their undisciplined behaviour
   b. Due to their disciplined behaviour
   c. Due to their mannered behaviour

B. Answer the following questions.

1. What do you understand by discipline?

____

____

2. How is discipline the basis of the whole universe?

____

____

3. Write the saying of Aristotle in your own words.

____

____

4. What happens when there is absence of discipline? What should be done to prevent decay?

____

____

5. Who become responsible adults?

____

____

6. What is the life-line of military departments? How?

____

____

7. What happens when there is lack of discipline in an army?

____

____

8. What is happening in the society due to lack of discipline?

____

9. What does discipline ensure?

____

10. Use these words in your own sentences.

Justice - ________________________________

Fair play - ________________________________

11. Find one from the lesson for each-

a. Common Noun - ____________________

b. Collective Noun - ____________________

c. Proper Noun - ____________________

d. Abstract Noun - ____________________

Creative Writing

C. Do you follow discipline at home and school? Write any three rules you follow yourself at both the places.

____

____

____

____

____

D. Do you also feel that people create chaos in public places due to lack of discipline?

____

____

____

____

Word Power

E. Write the pairs of antonyms in the given boxes.

Word Bank

unfair	fair	unity	guilty	cooperation
chaos	division	justice	order	disciplined
presence	desirable	injustice	absence	opposition
responsible	disordered	disadvantageous		

a. ____________ b. ____________ c. ____________

d. ____________ e. ____________ f. ____________

g. ____________ h. ____________ i. ____________

Grammar Skills

Simple Present Tense

Simple present tense is used

a. to describe repeated actions and habits.

b. to express facts which are true of all times.

c. to express a fact or something which is true at present.

d. to introduce a quotation

How to form simple present tense–

1. With **first person**, **second person** and all other **plural subjects**, we use **first** or **root form of the verb**.
2. With **third person**, **singular subjects** like he, she, it and all other **singular subjects**, we add **s/es** to the **first** or **root form of the verb**.

For example :

a. Cows **give** milk.

b. Rain **falls** from the sky.

c. Here **comes** my friend.

d. Wordsworth **says**, "Nature heals our negative mood."

F. Fill in the blanks with the simple present tense of the verbs given in the brackets.

The ostrich, which is now found only in African countries, is the largest living bird. It cannot (a) _______ (fly). But its powerful legs (b) _______ (carry) it at an amazing speed of about 50 km an hour. It (c) _______ (use) its feet to defend itself if it is unable to (d) _______ (get) away from its enemy. The ostrich is a tall bird. It (e) _______ (stand) almost two feet taller than an average man. It (f) _______ (has) only two toes; the head, neck and legs are almost bare. An ostrich (g) _______ (live) chiefly on fruits, grains, leaves and insects. They (h) _______ (swallow) small stones to (i) _______ (grind) their food with. People (j) _______ (raise) ostriches for their feathers.

Let us Know More

Discipline is highly useful in every walk of our life. We should follow it always whether we are in school, home, playground or any other place. It is a must for a happy and peaceful life. It gives us lots of opportunities, right ways to go ahead, to learn new things in life, to experience more within less time. Discipline is following the orders of our elders, teachers and parents who lead us towards success. We should value the importance of discipline in our daily life. People, who are not disciplined in their life, face lots of problems and get disappointment.

Fun Chat

Read the joke and laugh aloud.

Class Teacher : Your Maths are very poor. Why? Your science teacher has complained me.

Student *(innocently with tears in his eyes)* **:** Ma'am, if a single teacher can't teach us all the subjects, then how could you expect a single student to learn all the subjects?

☺ ☺ ☺

20 Home

Once, there lived a boy named Oliver. He was an intelligent boy. He was very good at sports. He did not like staying at home. He liked to play outside with his friends all the time. Whenever Oliver's parents would ask him to stay at home and spend time with his family, he would reply, "Staying at home is so boring."

One day, Oliver's mother decided to teach him a lesson. She thought of a plan. She shared her plan with Oliver's father, sister and grandparents. They all agreed to the plan.

One day, after sending Oliver to school, the entire family decided to go for a picnic. They left the keys with the **neighbour**.

When Oliver came back home, he saw the note at the door which said, "Keys are with the neighbour." Oliver took the keys and entered the empty house. There was nobody to welcome him with a smile. There was nobody to offer him a glass of water. Grandmother was not there to sit next to him while he would try to take a **nap**.

Oliver saw that his food was kept on the table. He did not feel like eating. He was missing all the members of his family.

He slowly got up from the table and walked towards his room. He sat there quietly. He said to himself, 'I am feeling so **lonely**. The house is so empty.'

Oliver could not sleep the entire afternoon. He kept missing his mom, dad, sister, grandmom and grandpa. He said to himself, 'A house is not a home without loved ones. A house becomes a home when all the members of the family live together in **harmony** and love.'

Know These Words

neighbour	-	a person living next door
nap	-	a light sleep
lonely	-	unhappy because you are not with other people
harmony	-	agreement

Questions-Answers

A. Underline the correct answer.

1. How was Oliver?

   a. Obedient   b. Intelligent   c. Smart

2. Who thought of a plan?

   a. Mother   b. Father   c. Sister

3. Where did the entire family decide to go?

   a. Hill station   b. Picnic   c. School

4. Where were the keys?

   a. With the neighbour

   b. Beneath the flower pot

   c. On the window sill

5. Oliver felt very ______ in the empty house.

   a. lonely   b. relaxed   c. peaceful

B. Answer the following questions.

1. What did Oliver like to do and why?

2. What did his parents ask him and what did he reply?

3. Who did Oliver's mother share her plan with?

4. What did Oliver see when he came back home?

5. What did Oliver see on the table? Did he eat?

6. What did Oliver say to himself at the end?

Creative Writing

C. Write in your own words what 'home' means to you.

D. How do you spend your time after studying?

Word Power

E. Complete the crossword puzzle using the clues given on the next page.

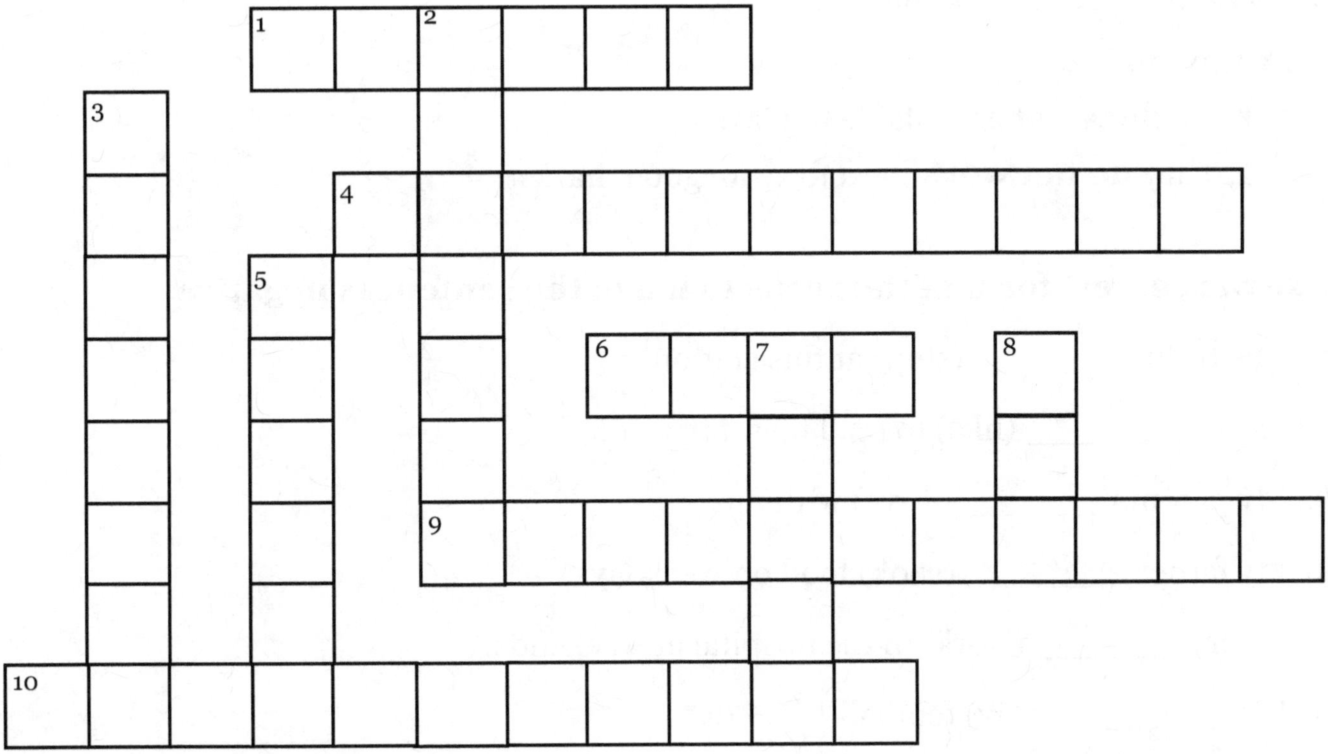

Across

1. the son of your sister
4. the mother of your father
6. the wife of your uncle
9. your brother's wife
10. the father of your father

Down

2. my father and my mother
3. a person's female child
5. a child of your uncle
7. the daughter of your brother
8. a person's male child

Grammar Skills

Simple Present Tense (Negative)

To form a negative present tense, we use **do not + verb** with a plural subject and **does not + verb** with a singular subject.

For example:

1. He **does not go** outside to play.
2. They **do not work** hard to score good marks.

F. Use the correct form of the verbs to make the sentences negative.

1. The train ________ (stop) at this station.
2. Sarah ________ (like) to read fairy tales.
3. My parents ________ (live) with me.
4. My father ________ (cook) food on weekdays.
5. Peter ________ (work) in the hospital at weekends.
6. We ________ (play) football.

7. Betty and Mary ________ (go) to bed early.

8. Children ________ (make) a lot of noise when the teacher is not there.

Let us Know More

There is no other better place in the world than being in the comfort of our home. Home is where we learn the first lesson of life. Unity, love and togetherness—all come from home. As the saying goes, "A house is built by hands, but a home is built by hearts." Home is where a heart lives. Home is the base for every individual and we should thank God for being blessed with a loveable home.

Fun Chat

Read the joke and laugh aloud.

Girl : Which is the strongest creature in the world?

Boy : The snail. It carries its whole house on its back.

☺ ☺ ☺

Boy : My father's name is Laughing and my mother's name is Smiling.

Teacher : So, you must be kidding.

Boy : No. Kidding is my brother. I'm Joking.

☺ ☺ ☺

21 Adventures

Adventures, adventures,
Are so much fun,
You can meet anyone,
You can take a **trip** to the Sun,
You never know what could be done.

How many, I don't know,
But there's more than one.

That is cool,
Or take a trip to the Moon,
Please come back sometime soon.

Go **as far as** I can see,
Let me suggest the stars are the
best most **definitely**,
But wherever you go you have to
let your mother know,

Now my poem is almost done,
Make sure to have fun.

Know These Words

adventure	-	an exciting experience
as far as	-	to the extent that
definitely	-	surely
definitely	-	surely

Questions-Answers

A. Fill in the blanks.

1. We can take a __________ to the Sun.
2. Stars look __________ in the sky.
3. We must let our __________ know where we are going.

B. Answer the following questions.

1. What are so much fun?

   ____

2. Which adventures are being talked about in the poem?

   ____

3. What is advised in the poem?

   ____

4. What should we do whenever we go outside?

   ____

5. Is meeting someone also an adventure that is mentioned in the poem?

   ____

6. What is suggested about the stars?

   ____

7. Use 'how many' in your own words.

   ____

8. Choose two conjunctions from the poem and use them in your own sentences.

   ____

Creative Writing

C. What activities do you find adventurous?

____

____

Word Power

D. Find the words (given in the Word Bank) in the word grid.

s	r	t	r	e	k	i	y	z	a	q
e	k	s	e	u	r	g	k	z	y	v
x	t	a	a	a	s	e	y	h	k	o
p	t	f	l	t	r	i	p	d	a	y
e	y	a	o	s	d	o	p	s	t	a
d	u	r	t	r	a	v	e	l	t	g
i	u	i	t	s	x	t	z	j	l	e
t	k	u	j	k	o	s	d	t	g	p
i	i	f	l	i	g	h	t	d	z	o
o	e	x	c	u	r	s	i	o	n	y
n	l	h	j	i	l	a	x	c	y	t

Word Bank

travel	voyage	expedition	excursion
safari	trek	flight	trip

Grammar Skills

Simple Past Tense

Simple past tense is used for describing an action in the past. We use **past form of the verb (II)** to make simple past tense.

For example:

William **studied** at night every day.

We **arrived** yesterday.

E. Read each of the following sentences. Underline the verb in simple present tense and rewrite the sentence in simple past tense.

1. The policeman catches the thief.

____

2. Liam finishes his work.

____

3. Our family plans a trip to Malaysia.

____

4. He lives here.

____

5. I get up at 6 o'clock.

____

6. Mr Sarah arrives at 9 o'clock.

____

7. It rains.

____

Let us Know More

We all must remember that—

1. Kids need the freedom to learn what life is like without a schedule.
2. Kids of all ages need a connection to Nature.
3. Kids need time to kick back and relax.
4. Kids need to figure out how to exist without technology.
5. Kids must be taught the importance of conservation.

Fun Chat

Interesting facts about moon:

- The Moon is Earth's only natural satellite and the fifth largest moon in the solar system.
- The Moon's presence helps stabilize our planet's wobble and moderate our climate.
- The Moon's distance from Earth is about 240,000 miles (385,000km).
- The Moon has a very thin atmosphere called an exosphere.
- The Moon's surface is cratered and pitted from comet and asteroid impacts.

22 Cooperation

Once, there was a smart boy named Noah. He studied in Class V. He was an intelligent boy. Everybody in the class liked him.

One day, there was a **competition** in his school. All the classes in the primary section had to make a chart for the Earth Day. Only one day was given for to them preparation.

Everybody wanted to win the competition. The **winning** class was to be taken out for a picnic by the class teacher.

In Noah's class, the teacher chose Noah to make the chart. Noah was a smart boy. So, he thought, 'If one person makes the chart, then the students of his class will miss their ideas.'

So, Noah decided to work together with the others. He asked everybody to give his ideas.

Many ideas came up. Then, Noah decided to put across the most popular idea on the chart.

He asked Lucas, "Will you draw the picture?" Lucas was **surprised**. He could not understand why Noah was asking him to draw the picture.

Noah said, "Lucas, the chart made by our class should win the first prize. The person, who is going to draw, should be the ablest to do it well. And you are the best artist in our class."

Lucas was very happy. He told Noah that he would need the help of the others as well.

The entire class worked as a team. Class V was awarded the first prize. The students were taken out for the picnic.

All the students understood the value of **cooperation**.

Know These Words

competition	-	an event where people try to win something
winning	-	top scoring
surprised	-	bewildered
cooperation	-	helpfulness

Questions-Answers

A. Tick (✓) the true statement and cross (×) the false one.

1. Noah was not liked by everybody. ☐
2. Noah asked Lucas to draw the picture. ☐
3. The entire class worked as a team. ☐
4. The students of class V were not taken out for the picnic. ☐
5. Noah was the best artist in the class. ☐

B. Answer the following questions.

1. What had to be done for the competition?

____

____

2. How did Noah plan to make a chart?

____

____

3. Where was the winning class to be taken?

____

____

4. Who did Noah ask for the drawing? Why?

____

____

5. Who was awarded the first prize and where were they taken?

____

____

6. What did all the students understand?

____

____

Creative Writing

C. Write any one of your experiences when you worked as a team to win a competition.

____

____

____

____

____

____

D. Write any three benefits of co-operation.

____

____

____

____

____

____

Word Power

E. Give each answer in one word.

1. The process of working together with a group of persons is called ______________.
2. The act of passing severe remarks and fault-finding is called ______________.

3. Speech or action intended to cause humiliation and laughter at a person to make fun of him is called ____________.
4. Idle talk about the personal or private affairs of others is called a ____________.
5. The imparting or interchange of thoughts, opinions or information by speech, writing, or by signs is called a ____________.
6. The voluntary arrangement in which two or more people engage in a mutually beneficial exchange is called ______________.

Grammar Skills

Simple Past Tense (Negative)

We use **did not** + **first form of verb** to make the negative sentences in past tense. It is applicable for all the singular and plural subjects.

For example:

Mr William **did not sell** his bike.

They **did not** write letters.

F. Change the following sentences into negatives.

1. He played cricket.

____

2. Nancy rode a horse lask week.

____

3. The Smiths built a big house.

____

4. Sarah and her friend drank a cup of tea.

____

5. Mum and I went shopping.

____

6. All the pupils stood up.

____

Let us Know More

Co-operation is a basic process of social life. Its nature is associative. Society cannot exist without cooperation. Human survival can be accomplished only if human beings act collectively. Society is produced by the cooperative activity of human beings.

Fun Chat

Read the sentences that show the murder of English and laugh aloud. Can you speak these sentences correctly?

1. Pick up the paper and fall in the dustbin.
2. I have two daughters both are girls.
3. Give me a blue pen of any colour.
4. The Principal is revolving in the corridor.
5. All of you stand in a straight circle.

23 Olympic Granny

When Grandma goes for gold in
The Olympic games this year,
She'll laugh at her competitors
And make them **quake** with fear.

She's ninety-nine years old
But, in athletics, she's been blessed,
The trouble is she can't decide
Which sport she plays the best.

She's such an **ace** at archery,
She's queen of the canoe,
She's tough to top at wonderland
And table tennis too.

She **dominates** the diving board.
She trumps the trampoline.
At lifting weights and wrestling
She's the best you've ever seen.

She speeds across the swimming pool
To **slake** the summer heat.
On BMX and mountain bike
She simply can't be beaten.

She's highest in the high jump,
And a **champ** at hammer throwing,

Magnificent in marathons,
Remarkable at rowing.

She beats the best at boxing,
At the pole vault she is **peerless**,
Her **fencing** is the finest;
She is positively fearless.

She's masterful at basketball,
She truly rules the court,
And equally **incredible**
At every other sport.

But what we find astonishing
And something of a **shocker**
Is how she wins all contests
With her wheelchair and her walker.

Know These Words

quake	-	shake
ace	-	expert
dominates	-	to have power and influence over others
slake	-	to quench
champ	-	a winner
peerless	-	matchless
fencing	-	the sport of fighting with swords
incredible	-	unbelievable
shocker	-	a person or thing that gives shock

Questions-Answers

A. Fill in the blanks.

1. Grandma will laugh at her __________.
2. Grandma is __________ in every game.
3. She is an ace at __________ .
4. She dominates the __________ and trumps the __________.
5. Grandma is positively __________ .

B. Answer the following questions.

1. Where does grandma go for the gold?

   ____

2. How old is grandma?

   ____

3. Of which sport is grandma is the queen?

   ____

4. In which sports can't grandma be beaten?

   ____

5. In what sport is grandma magnificent?

   ____

6. In what sport is grandma remarkable?

   ____

7. At which sport is grandma peerless?

   ____

8. At which sport is grandma masterful?

   ____

9. What is astonishing?

   ____

10. Choose and write all the action words from the poem.

____

11. Find the meanings of magnificient and remarkable.

____

Creative Writing

C. Do you have grandparents? What activities of your grandparents do you find amazing?

____

____

____

____

____

____

Word Power

D. Complete the crossword puzzle using the clues.

Across

4. This sport is played in a large open field where players can use only their feet to kick a ball into a goal.
7. This sport is played on the ice and the players use sticks to hit a puck into a goal.
8. This sport is played on a diamond-shaped field where players run the bases and score home runs.
9. This sport can be played on the beach where players hit a ball over a net.

Down

1. This sport is played with 10 players on the court. Players can shoot the ball into the hoop.
2. This sport is played with a racket and a yellow ball that players hit over a net.
3. This sport has many players on the field and on the sideline. They score touchdowns and kick field goals.
5. This sport is played outside where players hit a small white ball with a club.
6. This sport is played by throwing a ball down an alley. If you hit down all ten pins, you get a strike.

Grammar Skills

Simple Future Tense

Simple future tense denotes an action that will complete at some point in future time.

Use of Simple Future Tense

Simple future tense is used for describing an event or action in the future. We use **will/ shall** with the **first form** of the verb to make future tense.

1. Jack **will go** to Singapore tomorrow.
2. The meeting **will start** at 6 o'clock.

E. Use the verbs in the brackets to form simple future tense.

1. Sarah ________ to the cinema. (go)
2. Sandy ________ a novel. (write)
3. I ________ a famous singer. (become)

4. Mom _______ the clothes. (wash)
5. William _______ to school tomorrow. (go)
6. Dad _______ home at 9 o'clock. (arrive)
7. They _______ married in June. (get)
8. She _______ by bus. (travel)

Let us Know More

We all know that exercise is good for us. But it does more than just improving our physical fitness. It also reduces our risk of getting many diseases, such as cancer, heart disease or diabetes. It helps reduce stress, helps us sleep better and it improves our mental health as well. Since it does so much for us, it is important to exercise no matter what age we are. A lifelong exercise programme is the surest way to help us live and thrive into old age.

Path to Improve Health for Students

Exercise is good for you no matter how old you are. It helps children function better in school. It helps boost brain power as you age. It helps prevent falling ill when you are older. There is a place for exercise at every stage of a person's life.

Fun Chat

Sports Facts

The first modern Summer Olympics were held in Athens, in 1896.

The first Winter Olympics were held in Chamonix, France, in 1924.

The oldest Olympics medalist received his medal at the age of 33. His name was Anders Haugen and he was a ski jumper. He competed in 1924. Because of a scoring error he did not receive his bronze medal until 1974. 50 years later, he could receive it.

24 My Shadow

I have a little **shadow**
that goes in and out with me,
And what can be use of him
Is more than I can see.

He is very, very like me
from the heels up to the head;
And I see him jump before me,
When I jump into my bed.

The funniest thing about him
is the way he likes to grow.
Not at all like proper children.
Which is always very slow;

For he sometimes **shoots up**,
Taller like a rubber ball,
And he sometimes gets so little
that there's none of him at all.

Know These Words

shadow	-	a dark shape on a surface that is made when something stands between the light and the object
shoots up	-	increases very quickly and suddenly

Questions-Answers

A. Underline the correct answer.

1. What does go in and out with the poet?

   a. Friend b. Shadow c. Ball

2. What does the poet see the shadow doing?

   a. Jumping after him

   b. Jumping before him

   c. Jumping along with him

3. How does the shadow shoot up sometimes?

   a. Like a rubber ball b. like a star c. Like a tree

B. Answer the following questions.

1. Whom does a shadow resemble?

   ____

   ____

2. Do you also feel that shadow is just like you?

   ____

   ____

3. What is funniest about the shadow?

   ____

   ____

4. What happens when shadow gets very little?

   ____

   ____

5. Find a word in the superlative degree in the poem.

   ____

   ____

6 . Write the rhyming words for the following. (other than those mentioned in the poem)

a. me _____ _____   b. head _____ _____

c. grow _____ _____   d. ball _____ _____

Creative Writing

C. Have you ever observed your shadow at different times of the day? Write your observations telling the time when the shadow is longer and the time when the shadow is shorter.

____

____

____

Word Power

D. Find the given words (in Word Bank on the next page) in the word search.

w	t	r	a	n	s	p	a	r	e	n	t	z	r
r	r	r	s	j	b	p	r	i	s	m	a	t	e
c	t	a	o	o	a	e	m	i	t	i	b	r	f
r	s	i	i	h	t	c	y	u	c	o	s	a	r
e	r	n	p	n	m	z	u	i	z	p	o	n	a
f	i	b	c	c	a	y	i	v	r	t	r	s	c
l	o	o	b	e	n	u	o	t	p	z	b	l	t
e	f	w	r	n	s	t	a	r	k	o	c	u	i
c	u	r	z	a	s	h	a	d	o	w	j	c	o
t	k	z	t	i	g	h	t	u	z	j	k	e	n
y	o	c	o	l	o	u	r	i	h	o	o	n	y
s	r	s	p	e	c	t	r	u	m	l	k	t	s
d	o	l	u	m	i	n	e	s	c	e	n	t	u
o	p	a	q	u	e	q	u	e	o	p	c	k	n

Word Bank

reflect	prism	refraction	emit	translucent	colour
absorb	transparent	shadow	spectrum	tight	
sun	luminescent	opaque	rainbow	batman	

Grammar Skills

Present Continuous Tense

Present Continuous tense, also called present progressive tense, narrates an action which is being continued or going to be continued in the near future.

It is formed as follows :

Subject + is/am/are + –ing form of verb + ...

For Example : 1. Children are enjoying themselves at the picnic.

2. The traffic policeman is controlling the traffic.

3. I am revising my lesson.

E. Fill in each blank with the present continuous form of the verb given in the bracket.

1. The monkey ____________ the banana. (eat)
2. We ______________ to the movies. (go)
3. I _______________ the yoga class. (attend)
4. Soldiers _____________ the borders. (guard)
5. The child _____________ for milk (cry)

F. Fill in each blank with the correct form of the verb.

1. Mr William __________ (go) to office last week.
2. I __________ (take) 3 leaves from office every month.
3. They __________ (go) to London the next year.
4. The gardener __________ (water) the plants every day.
5. I __________ (buy) a new story-book yesterday.

6. Barking dogs seldom __________ (bite).

7. My classmate usually __________ (read) a story-book.

8. I __________(eat) pizza tomorrow.

9. He __________ (help) me in this project in the evening.

10. We __________(clean) all the windows of our house yesterday.

Let us Know More

A shadow happens when an object blocks the sun's rays. Shadows are longer in winter because of the angle of the sun. Your shadow is longest in the early morning and in the late afternoon. In the afternoon, when the sun is directly above you, your shadow leaves your side for a little while.

A long time ago, people observed the way shadows were formed by the sun and utilized this principle in making the world's most primitive clocks, the sundials.

Fun Chat

Riddles

Can you guess? All the riddles have the same answer .

A. What is as big as a cow but weighs nothing?

B. What is the same size and shape of an elephant but weighs nothing?

C. What's as big as a dinosaur but weighs nothing?

D. What's bigger than you, but doesn't weigh anything?

Answers

1.Good Manners

A. 1. a 2. c 3. a 4. a 5. a 6. a 7. a 8. a

B. 1. Manners make a person perfect and complete.
2. We should be respectful to our elders.
3. We should cooperate with each other in doing household work.
4. Good manners should be observed at school as well.
5. We should be polite even while turning down the unfair requests of others.
6. Whenever somebody does us a favour, we should thank him.

E.

				1 p				
			2 h	u	n	g	e	3 r
				r				e
			4 m	e	e	k		w
	5 m		e					a
6	o	o	r					r
	u		c		7 g	l	a	d
	r		y					
	n							

F. 1. a. Is this computer working?
b. This computer is not working.
c. Wow! This computer is working.

2. a. Are the buses running today?
b. The buses are running today.
c. Yeah! The buses are running today.

3. a. Do not hold my bag.
b. He holds my bag.
c. Can you hold my bag?

4. a. You are feeling sick.
b. Oh! You are feeling sick.
c. You are not feeling sick.

G. 1. The teachers are teaching in the class.
2. Switch on the fan.
3. There are many flowers in the garden.
4. My father was an enginear.
5. When did you go to the market?

2. Reading a Newspaper

A. 1. a 2. c 3. a 4. b

B. 1. Newspapers do us a great service by bringing us news from every corner of the world. We feel as if it has happened in our neighbourhood.
2. A politician finds the views and reviews of others on the policy adopted by the government of a political party.
3. A sports fan gets the latest information about his favourite game being played in any part of the world.
4. Sometimes newspapers become willing tools in the hands of vested interests.
5. We should prefer independent views and reviews while reading the facts given in the newspapers as they may not be true.

E. 1-f 2-e 3-a 4-b 5-c 6-d

F. 1-c 2-g 3-f 4-a 5-h 6-b 7-d 8-e

G. 1. Trees 2. World Teachers' Day 3. Rabbit 4. Weather 5. You

3. Health is Wealth

A. 1. a 2. b 3. a 4. c

B. 1. The king did not like to do anything because he was very lazy.
2. The king waited for his attendants to serve him every moment.
3. Eating good food and sleeping made him fat.
4. While conversing with each other, the holy man came to know that the king was unwell.
5. The holy man told the minister that he could cure the king.
6. The holy man brought out an iron ball of the size of a football and gave it to the attendants.
7. The Sadhu asked His Majesty that everyday morning and evening he had to roll that ball in the palace ground.
8. The holy man saw that the king had lost considerable amount of weight and was feeling much better and active.

E. 1. My	-	determiner	strawberry	-	noun
2. Johnson	-	noun	her	-	determiner
3. works	-	verb	hospital	-	noun
4. into	-	preposition	big	-	adjective
5. and	-	conjunction	gracefully	-	adverb
F. 1.Sure!	-	Interjection and conjunction	2. but	-	conjunction
3. in	-	preposition			

4. Mom

A. 1. tree 2. troubles 3. words
4. Mom, cares 5. best 6. Mom, dream

B. 1. He compares his mom to the sunlight in the first line.
2. Mom tells us not to fight and what is right.
3. She hears our screams without saying.
4. The poet is afraid of life.
5. The poet is looking for love.
6. The poet feels blessed that God has sent his mom for him from above.
7. wonderful, greatest

E. 1. Miss Suzie	-	proper,	house	-	common
2. team	-	collective			
3. Sundays	-	proper			
4. Mount Everest	-	Proper			
5. puppy	-	common			
6. colony	-	collective,	North	-	proper
7. Joseph	-	proper			
8. Jonson Street	-	proper			
9. band	-	collective			
10. houses	-	common			

5. Overcoming the Examination Stress

A. 1. c 2. b 3. a

B. 1. The most stressful time for students is when an examination approaches.
2. The great tension from teachers and parents stresses students to do well in the exam.
3. Those who are not well prepared for the exam suffer from anxiety and fear of failure.

4. The starting point to minimize the stress is to be attentive in the class as this is the most effective way of learning and understanding.
5. Students should be consistent in doing their homework and study steadily throughout the year without waiting for the exam.
6. Revision should be done regularly so that work may not get piled up.
7. Parents should help their children and monitor their progress in weak subjects.

E.

6 m	u	l	t	i	p	l	e	1 c	h	o	i	c	e	q	u	e	s	t	i	o	n
								a													
							5 a	n	s	w	e	r	s	h	e	e	t				
								d													
				4 e	x	a	m	i	n	e	r										
								d													
						3 e	x	a	m												
								t													
							2 c	e	r	t	i	f	i	c	a	t	e				

F. 1-j 2-e 3-a 4-i 5-b 6-h 7-d 8-g 9-f 10-c

G. 1-C 2-C 3-U 4-C 5-C 6-C 7-C 8-U 9-C 10-U

6. Presence of Mind

A. 1. b 2. a 3. b 4. a

B. 1. The bear said, "You have such a big farm and have grown a lot of things here, but you give me nothing to eat. It seems you are selfish. Now, I will destroy your farm."
2. The farmer said to the bear, "My family depends completely on this farm for a living. If you destroy it, we will all die of hunger."
3. The bear agreed not to destroy the crop on the condition that the farmer would share half the crop with him.
4. When the carrots were ripe for harvest, the wise farmer gave the bear all the leaves and kept the carrots for himself.
5. When by chance a few carrots slipped off the cart and the bear picked up a carrot and had a bite, it was very juicy and tasty. Then he tasted the leaves. They had no taste. Then he realised the cheating done by the farmer.
6. The farmer gave all the roots of wheat to the bear and kept the tops.
7. If the farmer had lost his presence of mind and had not used his wit, he would have been killed by the bear.

E. 1. essay 2. fail 3. result 4. test 5. examination
6. project 7. qualify 8. marks 9. pass 10. grade

F. 1. a 2. any 3. any, a 4. an 5. any, some
6. any 7. some 8. a 9. some 10. any

7. Show the Earth You Care

A 1. rivers 2. air 3. forest 4. bottles, cans

B. 1. The poem is indicating about the pollution on the earth.
2. We should remember that each of us must help keep the rivers clean, keep fresh the air we breathe and keep the forests green.
3. We should help others understand the effects of pollution in our life and tell them not to spread the litter everywhere.
4. The earth can be made pollution-free by not spreading the litter everywhere.
5. Litter
6. keep help recycle
7. Take time out for lunch. Work will still be here when you get back.
8. Bottles, cans, paper, plastic things, etc., should be recycled.

E.

F. 1. delievered transitive | 2. delievered intransitive
3. played transitive | 4. played intransitive
5. continue transitive | 6. continued intransitive
7. play transitive | 8. play intransitive
9. returned transitive | 10. returned intransitive
11. drinking transitive | 12. drinking intransitive

G. 1. write 2. were 3. appears 4. is 5. seem

8. Carefulness is the Key to Safety

A. 1. a 2. a 3. c 4. a

B. 1. A number of deaths occur as a result of road accidents.
2. The police say that most of the fatalities and injuries on roads are caused by the people driving their vehicles very fast.
3. Drivers do not observe their speed limits and make roads a dangerous place for all of us.
4. The number of accidents can greatly be reduced if drivers concentrate more on their driving.
5. In some countries, it is illegal to use a hand-held mobile phone while driving.
6. Cyclists can help themselves prevent these accidents by making themselves visible to motorists.
7. carefulness — Have patience, carefulness, strictness and strong responsibility.
carelessness — The loss resulting from carelessness is very serious.

E. 1. This
2. That
3. This
4. Those
5. That
6. Those
7. That
8. These

F.

p	r	o	t	e	c	t	i	v	e	p	y
t	a	y	y	h	u	y	a	a	u	r	a
s	l	r	c	a	r	e	f	u	l	e	v
q	a	s	i	r	o	u	s	y	s	v	o
m	r	u	o	m	t	i	q	l	t	e	i
s	m	i	p	l	e	o	r	o	r	n	d
z	e	o	s	e	c	u	r	e	q	t	a
j	d	s	e	s	r	p	y	n	s	a	b
k	a	k	t	s	t	o	u	e	a	b	l
c	o	n	t	r	o	l	l	a	b	l	e
s	t	d	s	v	a	d	i	d	s	e	s

Fun Chat

He is cleaning the windows from inside and when he falls, he falls, inside the house.

9. Florence Nightingale

A. 1. England 2. thoughtful, serious 3. 1853
4. nursing 5. Nightingale School of Nurses

B. 1. Florence Nightingale was born in 1820.
2. Her parents were there on a visit to the town of Florence in Italy at the time of her birth so they named her Florence.
3. She was distressed about the suffering of the sick and the poor. She felt that God wanted her to devote her life to serving them.
4. Florence Nightingale is best known for her services during the Crimean war.
5. Florence volunteered to go to the Eastern Europe with a group of nurses to take care of hundreds of soldiers wounded in the war.
6. It was common to see her carrying an oil lamp and walking through wards to make sure the patients had attention, they needed.
7. She was famous by the name "The Lady with the Lamp."
8. She gave talks on nursing at Nightingale School of Nurses at St. Thomas' Hospital, London.
9. Florence died in 1910.
10. Today, she continues to be a source of inspiration for nurses around the world.

D. 1. What is the colour of my pencil?
2. Who is responsible for the fault?
3. Where has Donna placed her English book?
4. Whose are these bags?
5. Who won the game yesterday?
6. Which is the biggest building in this area?
7. What does she want?
8. Whom did he tell this?

E. 1- b 2- e 3- d 4- h 5- c 6- a 7- g 8- f

10. Politeness

A. 1. a 2. b 3. c

B. 1. William was an ill-tempered and ill-mannered person.
2. When somebody gave him gifts, he would complain that it wasn't nice. Instead of saying 'thank you', he would hurt him/ her by saying harsh words.
3. The man at the counter was shocked at William's rudeness. He said. "The counter is closing.

I am sorry; I cannot give you any ticket."

4. He made a polite request to the person at the counter and got the tickets.
5. Daniel's bahaviour was very polite and respectful with the man at the counter.
6. William understood that when he was rude to people, he hurt them. It caused wounds in their hearts.

E. 1. rival — enemy
2. cleverness — wisdom
3. puzzle — confuse
4. obstinate — stubborn
5. roaming — travelling
6. talk — chat
7. existing — available

F. 1. blunt 2. entertaining 3. sad 4. poor
5. cruel 6. dishonest 7. helpful 8. satisfaction

G. 1. herself 2. himself 3. herself 4. themselves
5. himself 6. myself 7. itself 8. himself

11. Dreams

A. 1. images
2. imagination
3. sand
4. horrors

B. 1. Images of hope, fear, love and desire are locked up in our head.
2. Dreams are wishes that let our imagination grow. They let us travel anywhere at any time.
3. Dreams show us happy moments, our fears and love. They also tell us where from we should start.
4. Words and images that we see in our dreams swirl in our mind and let us express ourselves all the times.
5. Everything is softened by memories and dreams.
6. hope imagination
7. happiest
8. When he had a horror dream, he fell on his knees.
9. We are able to reach our heart and soul in our dreams.

E.

o	p	a	i	m	u	r	a	y	j	s	o
e	r	z	r	u	p	s	e	d	k	d	p
l	e	d	t	i	y	p	c	r	k	s	l
q	p	e	u	t	z	o	d	e	z	d	t
t	a	y	c	r	x	l	r	a	s	t	y
y	r	u	u	i	c	u	s	m	t	t	r
z	e	e	p	e	v	y	d	i	i	p	p
u	y	r	o	d	r	t	r	e	u	i	l
z	a	c	h	i	e	v	e	v	o	g	a
r	t	e	v	e	r	y	o	n	e	h	n
i	n	s	p	i	r	i	n	g	p	j	r

F. 1. a 2. a 3. a 4. an 5. an
6. a 7. an 8. an 9. a 10. a

12. Value of Good Health

A. 1. c 2. a 3. a 4. a

B. 1. Good health is a boon. It is the most precious possession of a man.
2. Only the man who has lost his health, can tell the value of good health.
3. Healthy minds can be found only in healthy bodies.
4. A man having good health, has healthy outlook towards life.
5. We should take only nutritious food for good health.

E. 1. Ingredient 2. overeating 3. diet
4. vitamins 5. overweight

F. 1. giant 2. blue 3. beautiful
4. red 5. small 6. sincere
7. black 8. round

13. Obedience

A. 1. b 2. a 3. c 4. b

B. 1. Jacob used to teach his sister to be obedient but she did not listen to him.
2. The fair had stalls of candies, soft drinks and ice creams. There were also stalls for children's books and toys.
3. On a bright Sunday morning, Jacob, Elie and their mom left for the fair.
4. Mom got worried when she realised that Elie was missing.
5. Jacob was waiting for her mom in the fair and it was getting dark.
6. Jacob's mom found Elie at a candy shop far away.
7. On seeing her mother she said, "I will always be obedient from now."

E. 1. awake 2. arrive 3. fastest 4. most
5. satisfied 6. wild 7. repair 8. careful
9. deep 10. soft

F. 1. five 2. few 3. many 4. many
5. few 6. all, less 7. enough 8. Every

14. The True Meaning of Life

A. 1. Years 2. moments 3. world 4. best 5. love

B. 1. The poet is writing the poem in his old age.
2. Many people came in the poet's life whom he loved very much. When they went away, the poet did not stop for them. He continued live and do his work.
3. No, the poet's life was not easy. He had to face many struggles in his life.
4. The nights were filled with tears.
5. The poet found that the things that seemed to him very important, were not so important and that's why he was not much happy.
6. Our opinion about ourselves and the feeling that we are the best, is really important according to the poet. The poet thinks that it is also important that how much kindness and love we can show to others before the end of our life.
7. The true measure of success is how much we helped the needy people.
8. plagued
9. many

E.

a	t	r	h	o	n	e	s	t	y	u	i	c	o	y	p
t	s	e	u	q	u	r	q	e	t	i	p	o	t	k	e
y	y	s	i	r	i	t	e	s	y	o	y	u	y	o	r
e	z	p	t	c	a	r	i	n	g	p	t	r	l	p	s
z	r	e	i	t	o	y	e	e	u	z	v	a	k	t	e
t	y	c	i	i	p	j	i	o	i	x	c	g	s	i	v
i	u	t	o	p	s	d	t	y	u	z	d	e	a	v	e
t	r	u	s	t	w	o	r	t	h	i	n	e	s	s	r
u	z	e	y	u	i	p	z	x	v	n	j	k	l	p	a
r	e	s	p	o	n	s	i	b	i	l	i	t	y	i	n
u	c	i	t	i	z	e	n	s	h	i	p	t	b	o	c
f	a	i	r	n	e	s	s	y	y	u	o	p	z	x	e
t	u	u	f	r	i	e	n	d	s	h	i	p	t	z	b

G. 1. This 2. those 3. that 4. this

5. these 6. this 7. that

15. Admitting Our Faults

A. 1. b 2. c

B. 1. Mistakes and failures are the foundations of a strong and bright future.
2. Failures are the pillars of success as we always learn from our mistakes.
3. The most difficult virtue to gain on the earth is to admit our own faults.
4. History enriches us with the knowledge to overcome the mistakes that we had committed in the past.
5. David had beautifully painted birds, mountains and animals on paper.
6. After realising his fault, he decided to practise painting on a board.
7. After years of practice and hard work, his efforts yielded him the fruit of success.
8. We should always admit our mistakes and try to learn from them.

E. a. hurt / injure b. loyal / faithful c. large / huge

d. sleepy / drowsy e. serious / grave

F. 1. early 2. today 3. late 4. yet 5. quickly

6. already 7. luckily 8. late 9. early 10. early

16. Advantages of the Cinema

A. 1. a 2. b 3. c 4. a 5. a

B. 1. The importance of the cinema is felt in all the spheres of life, such as educational, social, political and moral.

2. The cinema entertains us with interesting stories, melodious songs and enchanting dance.

3. We can learn about different parts of the country or the world.

4. No book can give any idea on geography of any country or town.

5. We can make the best use of films in imparting education to students.

6. Geography can nicely be taught by showing the illustrations of different landscapes, mountains, rivers, waterfalls, spring and different regions.

7. Films could make the people aware of keeping their streets and cities clean, fighting against diseases and living a happy life.

E. 1. manuscript 2. actor 3. film

4. producer 5. cameraman 6. box office

F. 1. upstairs: She had a room upstairs.

2. downstairs : She ran downstairs at once.

3. near : Come near and sit on this chair.

4. there : The remote is over there on the couch.

5. everywhere : I searched for my book everywhere.

6. out : we'll go out when the rain is over.

Fun chat : 1. The Godfather 2. Brave heart 3. Few Good Men

17. Trust

A. 1. a 2. a 3. b 4. b

B. 1. We can trust a friend who never proves to be ungrateful and treacherous.

2. The king started running to save his life from the mighty lion. In a flash, he climbed up a

tree to escape the lion.

3. The bear politely said, “Don’t be scared, O King! I will not harm you. Trust me. I am sitting on the tree to save my life from this wild lion.”
4. Realising that the king had slept, the lion began to convince the bear and said, “Push the king down; I will have my dinner and walk back to the den.”
5. The lion asked the king to push the bear down from the tree.

E.

	1 a											2 s	i	3 c	k
	n		4 h											o	
5 p	o	w	e	r	6 f	u	l					7 s	i	n	g
	i		a		a				8 p					f	
	n		l		i			9 t	r	o	u	b	l	e	
	t				t				a					s	
					10 h	a	p	p	y					s	

F. 1. rather 2. fairly 3. just 4. very 5. too
6. quite 7. almost 8. really 9. extremely 10. very

Fun chat : A promise

18. Steadfast Heart

A. 1. vanish 2. alone 3. fallen
4. disappointment, pain 5. enjoy

B. 1. No. Most of the dreams vanish at dawn.
2. He waits patiently for a long time, though he does not get the answers to all of his prayers but he gets inspiration to keep praying on.
3. Many friends left him to weep alone.
4. The poet describes that many of his friends are completely faithful who made him want to keep trusting friends.
5. The poet has held enough golden sheaves in his hands for sowing them for good crops.
6. The poet has enjoyed even the small things of life which he has compared to the roses.
7. The poem tells us to be always positive. It conveys that we should not get hurt with the things that do not happen in our life. But, we should always look at the things that God has made possible for us.

D.

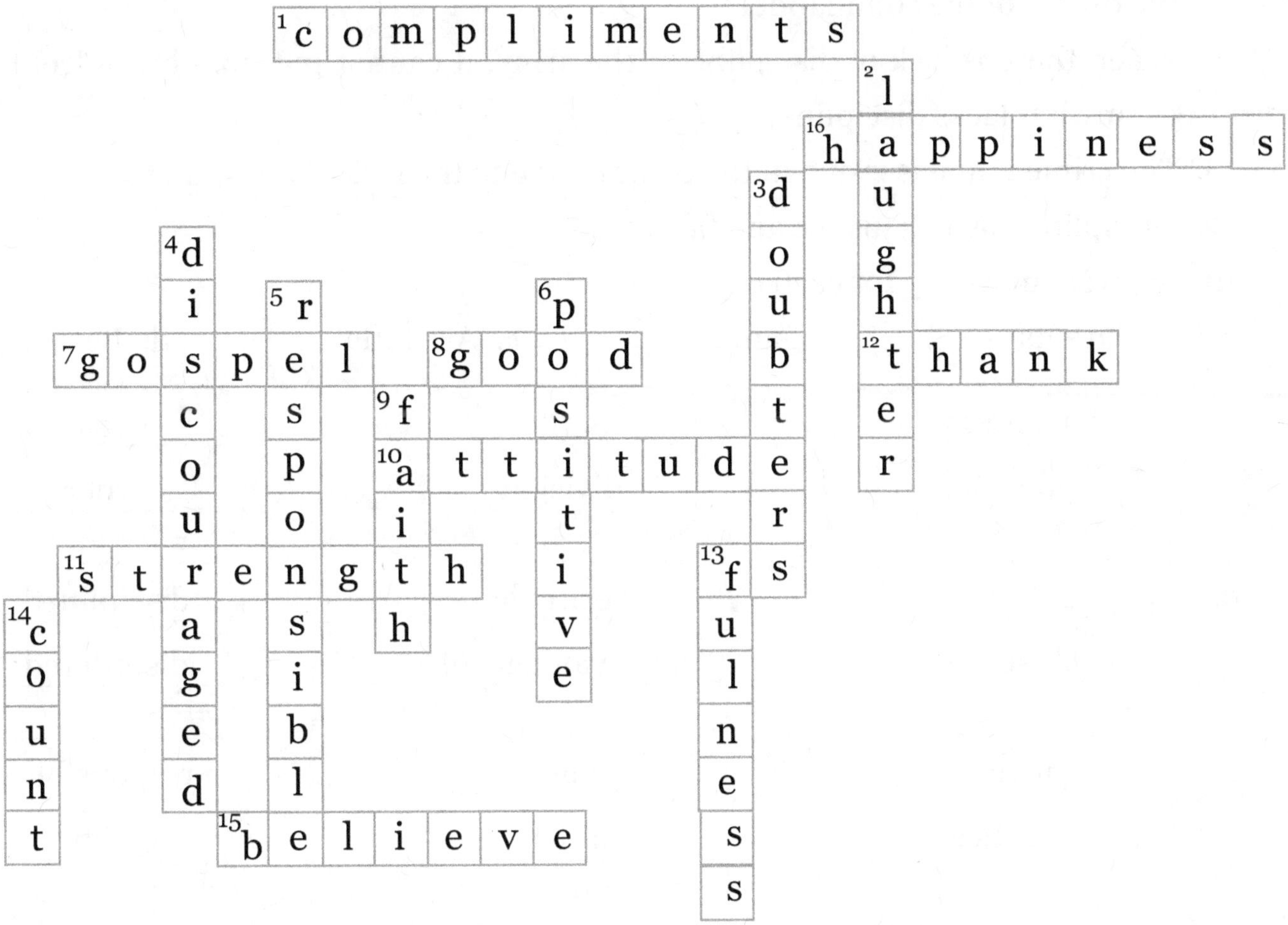

E. 1. usually 2. often 3. seldom
4. always 5. never 6. sometimes

19. Discipline Builds a Nation

A. 1. c 2. b 3. a 4. b 5. a

B. 1. Discipline is the process of training oneself in obedience, self-control and skill.
2. Discipline is the basis of the whole universe as the solar system is goverened by certain laws to maintain perfect harmony and beauty.
3. Everyone should follow rules made by the society in disciplined manner for the good of all the people of the society.
4. Absence of discipline means decay. To prevent decay, discipline has to be imposed in the common interest and for the common good.
5. Children growing in disciplined and happy homes become responsible adults.
6. Discipline is the lifeline of military departments. These armed forces follow a certain code of conduct. It demands loyalty to the country and to superior officers. It demands a spirit of fellowship and readiness to cope with an emergency. It is the duty of a soldier to obey

the orders of the commander.

7. When there is lack of discipline in the army, it cannot put up a brave front against the enemy if it lacks discipline.
8. The crime graph is rising in the country due to the lack of discipline.
9. Discipline ensures justice and fair play.
10. Answers may vary for each child.
11. a. Parents b. Family c. Aristotle d. Beauty

E.

a.	cooperation / opposition	b.	unity / division	c.	choas / order
d.	absence / presence	e.	desirable / disadvantageous	f.	disciplined / disordered
g.	justice / injustice	h.	fair / unfair	i.	responsible / guilty

F. a. fly b. carry c. uses d. get
e. stands f. has g. lives h. swallow
i. grind j. raise

20. Home

A. 1. b 2. a 3. b 4. a 5. a

B. 1. He liked to play outside with his friends all the time as he did not like staying at home.
2. Whenever Oliver's parents asked him to stay at home and spend time with the family, he replied, "Staying at home is so boring."
3. She shared her plan with Oliver's father, sister and grandparents.
4. When Oliver came back home, he saw the note at the door which said, "Keys are with the neighbour."
5. Oliver saw his food kept on the table. He did not feel like eating.
6. He said to himself, 'A house is not a home without loved ones. A house becomes a home when all the members of the family live together in harmony and love.'

E.

			1 n	e	2 p	h	e	w							
	3 d				a										
	a			4 g	r	a	n	d	m	o	t	h	e	r	
	u		5 c		e										
	g		o		n		6 a	u	7 n	t		8 s			
	h		u		t				i			o			
	t		s		9 s	i	s	t	e	r	i	n	l	a	w
	e		i						c						
10 g	r	a	n	d	f	a	t	h	e	r					

F. 1. does not stop
2. does not like
3. do not live
4. does not cook
5. does not work
6. do not play
7. do not go
8. do not make

21. Adventures

A. 1. trip
2. best
3. mother

B. 1. Adventures are so much fun.
2. A trip to the Sun and a trip to the Moon are being talked about in the poem.
3. It is advised to come back soon even though you have gone very far away.
4. Whenever we go outside, we should let our mother know about it.
5. Yes, it is also an adventure.
6. The poet has suggested that wandering in the stars is the best adventure.
7. How many stars are there in the sky?
8. 1. As far as – As far as I'm concerned, everything he says is a lie.
   2. Whenever – Whenever he leaves the house, he always carries an umbrella.

D.

s	r	t	r	e	k	i	y	z	a	q
e	k	s	e	u	r	g	k	z	y	v
x	t	a	a	a	s	e	y	h	k	o
p	t	f	l	t	r	i	p	d	a	y
e	y	a	o	s	d	o	p	s	t	a
d	u	r	t	r	a	v	e	l	t	g
i	u	i	t	s	x	t	z	j	l	e
t	k	u	j	k	o	s	d	t	g	p
i	i	f	l	i	g	h	t	d	z	o
o	e	x	c	u	r	s	i	o	n	y
n	l	h	j	i	l	a	x	c	y	t

E. 1. catches, The policeman caught the thief.
2. finishes, Liam finished his work.
3. plans, Our family planned a trip to Malaysia.
4. lives, He lived there.
5. get, I got up at 6 o'clock.
6. arrives, Mr. Sarah arrived at 9 o'clock.
7. rains, It rained.

22. Cooperation

A. 1. ✗ 2. ✓ 3. ✓ 4. ✗ 5. ✗

B. 1. All the classes in the primary section had to make a chart for the Earth Day for competition.
2. Noah decided to work together with the others. He asked everybody to give his ideas. Then, Noah decided to put across the most popular idea on the chart.

3. The winning class was to be taken out for a picnic by the class teacher.
4. Noah asked Lucas for drawing the picture because he was the best artist in the class.
5. Class V was awarded the first prize and the students were taken out for the picnic.
6. All the students understood the value of cooperation.

E. 1. team work 2. criticism 3. ridicule 4. gossip
5. communication 6. cooperation

F. 1. He did not play cricket.
2. Nancy did not ride a horse last week.
3. The Smiths did not build a big house.
4. Sarah and her friend did not drink a cup of tea.
5. Mum and I did not go shopping.
6. All the pupils did not stand up.

23. Olympic Granny

A. 1. competitors 2. best 3. archery
4. diving board, trophy 5. fearless

B. 1. Grandma goes to the Olympics for the gold.
2. She is ninety-nine years old.
3. She is the queen of the canoe.
4. She can't be beaten on BMX and mountain bike.
5. She is magnificient in marathons.
6. She is remarkable at rowing.
7. She is peerless at pole vault.
8. She is masterful at basketball.
9. Grandma is on her wheel chair and she walks with her walker, even though she wins all contests. This is very astonishing.
10. goes laugh
decide plays
dominates trumps
beats wins
11. a. attractive
b. amazing

D.

				1 b									
				a				2 t			3 f		
				4 s	o	c	c	e	r		o		
	5 g			k				n			o		6 b
7 h	o	c	k	e	y			n			t		o
	l			t				i			b		w
	f			b		8 b	a	s	e	b	a	l	l
				a							l		i
		9 v	o	l	l	e	y	b	a	l	l		n
				l									g

E. 1. will go 2. will write
3. shall become 4. will wash
5. will go 6. will arrive
7. will get 8. will travel

24. My Shadow

A. 1. b 2. b 3. a

B. 1. A shadow resembles the person to whom it belongs.
2. The answer may vary.
3. The funniest thing about the shadow is the way it grows.
4. It disappears.
5. Funniest
6. a. Bee b. bread
c. crow d. tall

D.

w	t	r	a	n	s	p	a	r	e	n	t	z	r
r	r	r	s	j	b	p	r	i	s	m	a	t	e
c	t	a	o	o	a	e	m	i	t	i	b	r	f
r	s	i	i	h	t	c	y	u	c	o	s	a	r
e	r	n	p	n	m	z	u	i	z	p	o	n	a
f	i	b	c	c	a	y	i	v	r	t	r	s	c
l	o	o	b	e	n	u	o	t	p	z	b	l	t
e	f	w	r	n	s	t	a	r	k	o	c	u	i
c	u	r	z	a	s	h	a	d	o	w	j	c	o
t	k	z	t	i	g	h	t	u	z	j	k	e	n
y	o	c	o	l	o	u	r	i	h	o	o	n	y
s	r	s	p	e	c	t	r	u	m	l	k	t	s
d	o	l	u	m	i	n	e	s	c	e	n	t	u
o	p	a	q	u	e	q	u	e	o	p	c	k	n

E. 1. is eating 2. are going 3. am attending

4. are guarding 5. is crying

F. 1. went 2. take 3. will go 4. waters

5. bought 6. bite 7. reads 8. shall eat

9. help 10. had cleaned

Fun chat : 1. shadow 2. shadow 3. shadow 4. shadow

NOTES

www.ingramcontent.com/pod-product-compliance
Lightning Source LLC
LaVergne TN
LVHW060451061126
851857LV00016B/1792